The Smart City Odyssey: Unveiling the Secrets to Traveller-Centric Software

John Shenton

Published by John Shenton, 2023.

While every precaution has been taken in the preparation of this book, the publisher assumes no responsibility for errors or omissions, or for damages resulting from the use of the information contained herein.

THE SMART CITY ODYSSEY: UNVEILING THE SECRETS TO TRAVELLER-CENTRIC SOFTWARE

First edition. May 24, 2023.

ISBN: 979-8227271624

Written by John Shenton.

Table of Contents

The Smart City Odyssey: Unveiling the Secrets to Traveller-Centric Software

PREFACE

As an industry professional with almost five decades of experience in designing, technical support, teaching, and programming computerized distribution, transit, and warehousing systems, I have been involved during the last 20 years of my career in architecting a traveller-centric software system using PHP and MySQL. Now that I am retired, I believe it is the perfect time to share my expertise and leverage a large amount of written material I wrote and accumulated during the architecting of a reservation and ticketing system for a smart city.

The purpose of this guide is to present thoughts and ideas on building a seamless sharing mobility on demand, Traveller-centric smart tourism platform for Smart Cities, providing tourists, locals, and travellers with full-course mobility service systems by designing and developing a smart city tourist and mobility software system. Its target audience includes developers, city planners, and policymakers who are enthusiastic about designing and implementing a similar system in their cities.

The guide commences by introducing the concept of smart cities and the pivotal role technology plays in transforming cities into smarter, more efficient entities. From there, it delves into the design requirements specific to a smart city tourist and mobility software system. This encompasses crucial aspects such as data collection and analysis, system integration, and the creation of a user-friendly interface.

The book provides a thorough overview of the various components that constitute the software system, including the tourist information system, public transportation, accommodation, traffic management, and other features like parking. Each component's design and functionality are examined in detail, emphasizing the unique attributes that render them suitable for a smart city environment.

In addition to addressing the technical aspects of development, the guide also tackles the challenges inherent in building such a system. It explores concerns related to privacy, cybersecurity threats, and the necessity for interoperability among different systems. Furthermore, I offer practical ideas for effectively addressing these challenges.

Ultimately, this guide aims to serve as an indispensable resource for individuals interested in constructing a smart city tourist and mobility software system. It presents a comprehensive, thought-provoking, and practical framework that empowers developers and city planners to create an efficient, user-friendly system that enhances the quality of life for both residents and visitors alike.

I hope this book not only enlightens readers but also inspires innovation and fosters the creation of smarter cities worldwide.

John Shenton - June 2023

Transforming Urban Living: The Intersection of Smart Cities and On-Demand Mobility

Our cities are ever expanding. Around four billion people in the world live in urban areas, and it is projected that by the year 2030, there will be forty-one megacities across the globe-each of which will be home to more than 10 million people.

A smart city is an urban area where technology is rooted within the very heart of the destination. This technology is put in place to improve the interior workings of the city, from its transport and its traffic control to its energy management. This not only makes the city a better environment for its inhabitants but an easier destination for tourists to travel to navigate around. These benefits and developments are turning smart cities into smart tourist destinations, and they are starting to change the way we travel across the globe.

The way we move around our cities is one of the most crucial aspects of being an urban dweller. Many city transport systems are increasingly under strain, but Mobility on Demand (MOD) combining traditional public transportation with private enterprise options into a single mobility service offers a solution. By allowing passengers to move around the transport network more freely, mobile ticketing solutions are the future of speedy travel and stress-free transport.

As our cities expand and their existing infrastructure is put under increased pressure, the need for smart and innovative solutions to deal with this growth in mobility is ever greater. Smart technology with the fast development of information technologies and telecommunication systems contributes to consistent changes in the transit, travel, and tourism industry including destination management. The wide introduction of new technologies and software comprises an integral part of the strategic business development of companies operating in these industries. Destination management software technology is a prospective direction for the development of business in the field of tourism and travel, but companies and customers should come prepared to use the full potential of such software technology.

Smart Destination Management Software Technology

In actuality, there are destination management software technologies available to both companies and customers, which facilitate the development of destination management for companies and customize travel and tourism planning for consumers. At this point, consideration should be given to a Traveller-centric Reservation system, which offers customers not only opportunities for the reservation or booking of tickets or hotels but also provides a multi-platform software framework, around which customers can construct and plan their travel or vacations. The distinct feature of destination management software technology is the ability to consolidate and distribute a comprehensive range of travel and tourism products through a variety of platforms, which are elaborated for the specific region or service. In this regard, the use of destination software management technology facilitates the identification of the key requirements of customers to offer them the mobile and fixed services, they need.

At this point, it is worth mentioning the fact that destination management software technology involves enterprise software linked to service providers and customers. The enterprise software turns out to be a sort of mediator between service providers and customers, while the enterprise uses the software to process the information and deliver it in a plausible form to customers. For example, a company can obtain information about available travel requirements, hotels, tours, transfers, restaurants, and other services, which customers are looking for. The enterprise software does not provide a unique offer to customers, which they have to accept or reject. Instead, the enterprise software provides them with a choice of a variety of services the enterprise can offer using its service suppliers, while customers can choose the ones, which meet their interests the most. In such a way, the company providing travel, tourism, and destination management services can benefit from the high level of customer satisfaction, while customers benefit from the availability of a variety of services, which they can choose using the enterprise software.

Traveller-centric Mobility on Demand

The concept of Traveller-centric revolves around empowering consumers with flexible mobility packages through a single, comprehensive app. Passenger transportation encompasses a diverse range of transport modes and operations, none of which can single-handedly offer a complete set of mobility solutions.

In the realm of Mobility as a Service (Traveller-centric) platforms, digital platforms play a pivotal role in supporting end-to-end trip planning, electronic ticketing, and payment services across both public and private transportation options. This necessitates a solution that incorporates real devices, actual browsers, and an overlay of user conditions that cannot be replicated elsewhere. A Traveller-centric system serves as a capable demand response platform, augmenting the mobile backend integration of small or medium-sized transit agencies.

Connected mobility emerges as a solution by harnessing the vast amount of data it gathers. By leveraging this data, Traveller-centric platforms can address the challenge of integrating various modes of transportation seamlessly. This results in improved access to transport expanded transportation options, and the elimination of time-consuming inconveniences associated with locating, coordinating, booking, and paying for each mode of transportation individually.

With Traveller-centric platforms, it becomes possible to bridge the gap between the first and last mile of a passenger's journey. These platforms offer appropriate transit options tailored to a specific point in time, encompassing services like Uber, Lyft, carpooling, ride-sharing, bicycles, and scooters. This comprehensive approach ensures that passengers have access to the most suitable mode of transit for their specific needs, enhancing their overall travel experience.

Enterprise Software Technology

As such, enterprise software technology helps to build stronger company-customer relationships on the ground of the high level of customer satisfaction and attractive technologies available to the customer. At the same time, the enterprise software may be used by different companies operating in the tourism and travel industry since they can install the software and use it to process information available to them from their suppliers and provide their potential customers with the opportunity to make reservations and plan their trips and recreation accurately.

Enterprise software contributes to the improvement of the quality of services provided by companies that use the software because this software enhances the quality of information processing, and increases the speed of information processing and delivery of the information to customers. Customers, in their turn, enjoy the multi-platform nature of the software, which expands the scope of the application of software and its use by customers.

Thus, enterprise software contributes to the overall improvement of the quality of services provided by companies operating in the tourism and travel industry to customers. In addition, the software opens wider choices in the face of customers which is very important for customers, who want to customize their travel.

Collaborative Economies in Smart Cities: Maximizing Shared Benefits

The sharing economy – also known as collaborative consumption – is a peer-to-peer marketplace in which suppliers (everyday people) exchange or rent out excess capacity (e.g., sleeping facilities, a room on a yacht, or even an evening meal).

While the sharing economy does involve sharing, it also involves commercial transactions – i.e., the use of excess capacity in exchange for remuneration.

There does not appear to be a single definition, as the sharing economy can be business-to-business, collaborative, peer-to-peer or peer to crowd, etc.

Many describe the new-shared economy marketplace as one that allows services to be provided on a peer-to-peer or shared-user basis. This type of sharing our exchange of goods or services is generally facilitated by online digital platforms that match demand and supply, such as:

• Airbnb – short-term accommodation rental and travel experiences platform,
 • Homeaway – vacation rental platform,
 • Uber – short-distance ride-sharing platform,
 • EatWith – shared dining platform,
 • Vayable – personal tours and travel experiences platform,
 • ToursByLocals – private tours platform

So, the question is how does your business and its current technology utilize or enter into the sharing economy?

For this particular discussion, we will concern ourselves with reservation and ticketing concerns for tourism and transportation companies existing and operating within a smart city. Tourism as in activities, rentals, campgrounds, etc. Transportation primarily for small bus lines, shuttle companies, water taxis, and smaller ferry operations.

Typically, the majority of these companies use fairly basic reservation systems that purely cope with the ability to take online reservations, receive payment and produce the appropriate tickets and invoicing information for their clients.

But, as technology and the sharing economy benefits B2B businesses, it challenges smaller operations to come up with innovative solutions.

Internet of Things (IoT), Cloud Computing, Data-Sharing, and many other technical buzzwords have made their entrance into the modern lexicon, they are in effect forcing the entrepreneurial universe to all new levels.

What we are seeing in effect is that large organizations are taking over the sharing economy and leaving smaller individual businesses to either accept reservations being taken on their behalf through the large shared digital platforms or pay appropriate fees and commissions to those platforms.

Or, continuing to carry on business as usual and accepting these costs as part of doing business.

We feel that there is an alternative. Although many businesses are used to thinking of the sharing economy as being peer-to-peer (P2P), in reality, we find there are at least three common platforms in use: Business to business (B2B), business-to-consumer (B2C, also known as business-to-crowd), and P2P.

This is where a Traveller-centric digital reservation and ticketing-sharing platform is best suited. It easily satisfies all of the above scenarios in a single-sharing system.

It easily allows a single website to embrace a collaborative business model. Let us for instance look at an activity-related website. Using standard tour reservation software, one can only take reservations for those tours, etc. This leaves the website owner at the mercy of large sharing platforms, with their attendant large SEO budgets and ability to reach and offer consumers multiple activity offerings.

With Traveller-centric, you can establish a sharing platform whereby not only do you take reservations for your activities, but you can offer smaller non-competitors of tourism-related products and offerings within your destination the ability to share and take orders from your website.

Not only does this increase the capabilities and profitability of your activity reservation website, but it allows you to become part of the sharing economy using its multi-tenant and multi-website capabilities.

Business Impact: For many collaborative consumption activities, such as bicycle- or boat-sharing, the economic impact is simply additional consumption reflected in the GNP.

Other sharing services are, economically, a zero-sum game in which the sharing service (with remuneration) acts as an alternative to a previously paid service. It is safe to say that collaborative consumption both cannibalizes existing businesses and creates new demand.

Technology: The sharing economy is not new, but new technologies and perspectives allied with multi-tenant, multi-site systems such as Traveller-centric systems have given impetus to the rise in collaborative consumption driven by the convergence of specific societal, economic, and technological factors.

The technological influences are:

- Mobile devices and platforms
- Social networking
- Online payment systems (e.g., PayPal)

To satisfy customers, travel companies (specifically OTA's and GDS) need to participate in the collaborative economy, either as suppliers or facilitators of shared content and to automate payments and expense reporting to attract business travellers as part of local, regional, and global partnership opportunities and also there is the potential for worldwide distribution deals.

OTA's could join forces with sharing services to provide distribution, and points of sale (e.g., travel agents), with technology platforms that support cloud-based inventory and content management, such as Traveller-centric Voyager.

Reservation and Ticketing Technology for the Sharing Economy

Before the advent of the sharing economy, tourism services had traditionally been provided by businesses such as hotels, shuttle companies, taxis, or tour operators. Ticketing for transportation and also for the tourism industry in general, have also been part of that equation.

In recent years, a growing number of individuals have begun to share what they own temporarily with tourists, for example, houses, other accommodations, cars, etc. This has also grown to include meals or exclusions.

This type of sharing is referred to as the sharing economy. Although it is not limited to tourism, it is now found in many areas of social and economic activity, with tourism being one of the sectors most impacted.

The sharing economy with its values of collaboration, cooperation, and partnership is changing the tourism and transportation marketplace. By providing people with new options for where to stay, what to do, and how to get around, it would appear that in a sharing economy, anyone can start a tourism or transportation business.

Digital Platform Models and the Sharing Economy

With the rise of smart cities, Digital Platform Business Models, and the Internet of Things (IoT) we are beginning to see significant changes in productivity, lifestyles, and business models. Yet, companies are still grappling with the changes to consumer-facing applications and navigating the data they produce.

Travellers are beginning to feel the true power of mobile and other disruptive technologies and what they offer to the travellers' experience. Until now, only the majority of travel suppliers such as hotels and airlines offered basic functionality, including flight and hotel check-ins, boarding passes, itinerary updates, and shopping with booking capability.

This confluence of technologies, with its cloud computing, increased processing power, (IoT), etc. has begun to push mobile channels into hitherto unthought-of areas of travel and improve the overall trip experience.

Now more than ever, travel companies and tourist destinations, aligned with transportation, hotels, flight, and activity providers are giving unprecedented attention to providing an end-to-end consumer travel experience.

Companies involved in the tourist and transportation arena, need to engage with potential customers from their early thoughts on taking a vacation, to booking, to their ride to and from the airport, flights, accommodation, and finally what activities they partake in once they arrived at their destination.

The accommodation and airline industry have already made inroads into ensuring that accommodation and flights have become a commodity transacted over the Internet with its attendant depression of gross margins to the smaller accommodation providers, etc.

When we analyze and study a large number of ground transportation providers at major destinations it can be seen that it remains a fragmented and somewhat challenging part of the seamless travel experience.

More and more we are seeing individual activity and transportation websites being overtaken and supplanted by newer transportation startups such as Uber, Lyft, etc.

These companies currently are almost exclusively seeking travellers in the highly lucrative on-demand market. The other side of this ground transportation coin is the multibillion-dollar industry of prebuilt transportation.

Also at destinations and other tourist locations, we have a wide range of activity providers. Typically each activity provider has its unique website being marketed specifically for its activity.

To progress in providing maximum consumer benefit and withstanding the coming industry disruption from other major players, such as Amazon, Google, and Microsoft, etc., and subsequent depression of margins as seen in the accommodation and flight booking arena, then companies need to be looking forwards also into the sharing economy.

One of the most cost-effective entry points into the sharing online economy is by implementing and digitizing mobility solutions with platform-based business models.

Creating a Digital Platform

A digital platform-based business model creates value by connecting individuals or companies. As previously mentioned with Uber, Amazon, etc. these types of businesses are becoming more common through the evolution of the Internet and are operating from platform-based models.

According to Forrester, the digital platform companies that collectively make up the sharing economy represent a $100 billion market.

A platform business model is a plan for creating revenue by allowing registered members or suppliers to create product content that can be consumed by a specific user group or general audience.

A platform can either provide open APIs or integrate other APIs to provide external developers with the ability to expand the platform's functionality by allowing other application programs to interact and share data.

Creating a multi-tenant, multi-supplier ecosystem that encourages registered users and product consumers to add more value to that platform will, in turn, attract additional product content creators and consumers.

As such a platform develops more connections to mobile and Internet of Things devices, they must be based on open standards and APIs to make the platform shareable and attractive to ecosystem partners.

Thus, they will need to be based on a cloud/hybrid cloud foundation that is technically designed to scale with the network's effect on the ecosystem.

What are your cities or company's current digital technology capabilities? Are there gaps in your existing website that need to be filled or redesigned to become a platform ecosystem?

Then, if you are seeking a purpose-built, scalable business model for collective, collaborative, and enterprise growth, it's the perfect time to get started with Traveller-centric, agile, scalable, tourism and transportation software platform.

Hybrid Business Ecosystems for Smart Cities

It is generally considered that the main components of tourism are accessibility, accommodation, and attraction or locale. Typically these are considered the three A's of tourism.

Thus, a smart business ecosystem enabling the exchange of tourism resources and tourism experiences should include a fully integrated and dynamically interconnected digitalization of these core business processes.

As the web has become the major medium through which tourists and destination stakeholders interact and collaborate, exchanging information, knowledge, and product to display a common destination vision.

As such, a destination needs to become a network of connected organizations that are either directly or indirectly related to terrorism, and such a network requires a technological infrastructure aimed at creating a digital environment that will support cooperation and product sharing.

The business ecosystem would need to include reservation capabilities for one of the main components of terrorism, which is accessibility. Or, how do we get there?

The above mostly includes transportation, which needs to be regularly scheduled, economical, comfortable, and secure. Depending upon the destination, this includes boats and ships, cars and buses, trains, and aviation.

Another component of the business ecosystem for tourism would be accommodation. Tourists would require a place to stay upon reaching the destination and the means to get food. As with accessibility, an accommodation requirement also needs to be economical, comfortable, and secure.

Such accommodation would also vary according to the tourist destination. Ranging from luxury hotels to campgrounds and RV parks, etc.

One could argue that the third and most important component of any tourist destination is the list of attractions. Attractions are those elements, which determine the choice of tourists.

These attractions spur the desire to travel and motivate travel. Attractions may be natural attractions, event attractions, built-in attractions, and cultural and social attractions.

All of the above require their unique ability to take a reservation, payment, invoice, and ticket issuance for any of the selected travel products available at a destination.

A smart tourism business ecosystem at the destination needs to facilitate the process of integration between production and consumption and increase linkages between suppliers and consumers of a tourism product.

One could define a tourism product as a bundle or package of tangible and intangible components based on activities at a destination.

For the tourist, this package is perceived as an experience available at a price.

As such, the destination requires a system that fully integrates passenger transport reservation and ticketing capabilities, accommodation and rental components, activity and event ticketing capabilities, e-commerce, and more.

All of the above are bundled into a fully integrated smart tourism web-based business ecosystem.

Also, with the disparate number of suppliers of tourism products at a destination, one can easily see why hybrid technology software would be envisaged to integrate with both legacy and new technology systems already installed.

A Traveller-centric-digital-ecosystem is such a hybrid technology for tourism and destination websites.

Shaping Tomorrow's Cities: Harnessing the Potential of Smart City Digital Tenants

Building a smart city hybrid cloud ecosystem of reservations, transportation, and ticketing companies from a single installation of a Traveller-centric designed software system.

Multi-Tenancy

Multi-tenancy is a highly effective business strategy that empowers Transportation, Reservations & Ticketing companies to serve multiple customers, or "tenants," through a single instance of their software application. This approach offers tremendous advantages within the context of the Transportation, Reservations & Ticketing industry, enabling businesses to provide tenants with the ability to share and personalize various sections of their comprehensive solution.

In a multi-tenant architecture, each customer shares the same software application and utilizes a single database. To ensure data integrity and separation, the information stored in the database is appropriately tagged to identify its ownership by specific customers. The software itself is intelligently designed to discern and handle the data belonging to each tenant.

The key advantage of a multi-tenanted software architecture lies in its ability to serve multiple customers efficiently from a single application instance operating on a solitary server or a pool of servers. This stands in stark contrast to a single-tenant approach, where each customer would require a dedicated software instance running on dedicated servers. By consolidating resources and infrastructure, multi-tenancy allows for streamlined operations, reduced costs, and simplified maintenance and upgrades.

Moreover, for small business owners utilizing Traveller-centric systems, multi-tenancy offers an opportunity to leverage peer-to-peer and B2B marketplaces on their terms. Through collaborative consumption, these businesses can expand their offerings by incorporating additional products and services on their websites, thereby facilitating growth and enhancing their companies' value proposition. This approach opens doors for partnerships and synergies, enabling businesses to tap into a wider customer base and cater to diverse needs, ultimately boosting their competitive edge and market presence.

By embracing a multi-tenant strategy, a Traveller-centric Transportation, Reservations & Ticketing business can unlock new avenues for innovation, customization, and collaboration. This approach maximizes efficiency, fosters scalability, and positions companies for long-term success in a rapidly evolving industry.

Single-tenancy

A single instance of the software and the entire supporting infrastructure serves a single customer. With single tenancy, customers have their independent database and instance of the software. With this option, there's essentially no sharing going on. Everyone has their own, separate from everyone else.

Creating Urban Experiences of Tomorrow: Innovative Destination Management Systems

Destination Management Systems are systems that can consolidate and distribute a comprehensive range of tourism products through a variety of channels and platforms, generally catering to a specific region, and supporting the activities of a destination management organization within that region.

A DMS can utilize a customer-centric approach to manage and market the destination as a holistic entity, typically providing strong destination-related information, real-time reservations, destination management tools and paying particular attention to supporting small and independent tourism suppliers.

You should be thinking of features of a multitude of the latest technologies and APIs. Among these, are tour, accommodation, hotel, rental, shuttle, campground, RV trailer park, ferry, bus, event manager, restaurant and other powerful, fully integrated eCommerce solutions.

Complex Inventory Management

Traveller-centric systems empower users to create, price, allocate and modify inventory in real-time with its integrated real-time inventory management system.

Traveller-centric enables management of information in real-time; reservations, dynamic pricing, inventory availability and related ancillary services with integrated processing of sales through the web.

Thereby creating a complete distribution management system that offers control over how products and services are offered and sold. Online shoppers can check available inventory and complete a reservation online making the experience more efficient and less time-consuming.

To this foundation, we added user-defined item level occupancy and pricing control, event, category and item level fee assignment, in-depth discount calculation and application, and online credit card transaction processing.

Dynamic item-level pricing based on user-defined business rules and configuration. Multi-tier inventory management, dimensional pricing, user-defined business rules, fees, discounts, and much, much more.

Further, within an integrated rental module, you can define rental prices at the category, subcategory, or even single product level. Also, set rental pricing for different seasons and switch between them with a few clicks

Event creation is simplified through templates and the ability to clone entire events, categories or individual items.

Traveller-centric's inventory and distribution capability successfully integrate all the features needed by travel distributors, for all travel services: Traveller-centric is ideal for tour operators that design and build their packages (holidays, tours, city breaks, trips etc.), and resell other services and packages from third party tour operators – and who require a way to manage availability, inventory, and prices.

Traveller-centric is entirely roles and permissions based allowing you to define authorities and access at the individual user level.

Passenger Inventory Management

It provides the key functionality for reservations and inventory control, trip and schedule management, in conjunction with associated pricing, ticketing and check-in.

Traveller-centric Reservations can manage bookings made at local and partner sales offices, through travel distributors, and online sites.

Traveller-centric Passenger Management and Distribution offer the most comprehensive range of passenger management services available.

Its infrastructure is built on a flexible platform of core system features required by every transit company, including reservations, ticketing, inventory, check-in, departure control and weight and balance.

It is a modular software suite for reservation and multi-channel ticket distribution.

The system handles multi-segment and multi-stopover passenger transport services, with or without reservation including sales of additional on-board services and after-sales operations of previously created bookings.

Traveller-centric supports many major ticketing strategies and methods of passenger transportation, such as no-sale-block adjustment, ticket pre-allocation, inventory sharing as well as inventory re-use.

Accommodation, transport, transfer and additional services can be chosen for custom packages, based on the links, rules and restrictions that you set up. You can model the dynamic packages on the fly, by adding or removing restrictions among services while on sale.

You can join services statically, under fixed, predefined packages or dynamically create packages by linking different travel services.

As well, it supports you in all your task management: from prices by product and product type to load factor to dates and other factors. Moreover, it also lets you buy and sell live inventory across multiple channels – and take advantage of your purchasing power and distribute through your preferred channels.

Passenger Management and Distribution

Traveller-centric Passenger Management and Distribution include technologies to optimize your customer service – including online, kiosk and mobile applications, self-service booking, shopping solutions, merchandising and loyalty programs.

It also features an interface for third-party distribution, enabling you to work seamlessly with all your partners.

1. A solution that updates inventory across all channels as

transactions happen.

2. It also supports multichannel order management and multichannel distribution.

With the modular integration capabilities loading, you can centralize all of your different sales channels and websites. They provide you with a unified view of all of your orders, despite their origin or order type.

Today's tourism market represents the ideal sector in which Traveller-centric smart solutions can be implemented. From the notion of a 'Smart City,' we move on to its derivate – 'Smart Tourism' and 'Smart Destination'.

The capability of Traveller-centric to integrate on a modular basis, many facets of a city's reservation and ticketing requirements, ranging from passenger transport, accommodation, rentals, parking and activity-related endeavours, allows it to cover most destination-based multiple passenger and tourism activities.

Its multi-tenant, multisite capabilities provide your distributors with the power to engage their customers with your packaged vacation products— effectively maximizing your overall profitability and expanding your online reach. Create your online destination marketplace, allowing vendors and partners to manage their travel products on your Transportation, Reservations & Ticketing websites.

Electronic Customer Relationship Management (eCRM)

The key to meeting today's customer's expectations is 'Electronic Customer Relationship Management (CRM) an approach that integrates all of your customer information and makes it available for each customer contact, so you can provide the kind of consistent and effective personalized service customers want.

It need not be expensive for a small to mid-sized company as it is not primarily a single technology, but a refocusing of an organization's collection and use of customer data using existing technologies.

Although companies selling unified e-CRM solutions may dispute this point.

The goal of e-CRM is to serve the same essential purpose of customer service in any business. That is, understand who your customers are and what they want. The challenge for e-business is to quickly merge your information from a variety of diverse sources into a sales face that can provide your customer with the comforts of shopping environments with which they are already familiar.

My research of client requirements over the many years has resulted in identifying a few key details that are sometimes missed when researching reservation software solutions.

The main detail is, that the majority of tour reservation software and other reservation software on the market that are provided as a hosted SaaS solution does not have any real CRM capabilities other than maintaining a client database.

Also, as the reservation software database is hosted in a shared environment and served as a service, it is not necessarily under the client's direct control and as a consequence does not provide sufficient information that is useful on a relationship basis.

Reservation software, such as Traveller-centric Enterprise with its customer relationship management capabilities and the fact that it can be installed directly on the customer's website server, means that not only is customer information secure and controlled by the client, but it also contains a wealth of information that can be used to increase a client sales and profitability.

Traveller-centric Enterprise contains a wide variety of customer relationship material. It is wide-ranging from detailed customer files, sales information; loyalty rewards points, items purchased and so much more.

Traveller-centric Enterprise Electronic Customer Relationship Management (CRM) in Reservation Software integration provides a solution that brings them all together for every customer contact.

e-CRM will enable your companies marketing department to identify and target your best customers, manage marketing campaigns with clear goals and objectives, improve telesales, account, and sales management, generate quality leads for the sales team to identify the most profitable customers and provide them with the highest level of service.

Business Process and Rules Management

A smart city's traveller-centric system should be equipped with a powerful 'Business Meta Rule Engine' designed to empower users in swiftly implementing complex business processes as part of its comprehensive decision support system. This advanced engine enables customers not only to book their travel in advance but also provides them with a transparent view of price variations across different sailings. By doing so, it incentivizes customers to choose less busy sailings, optimizing equipment capacity utilization for transit companies.

Moreover, the system must offer analytical capabilities essential for effectively managing yield and capacity through features like failure analysis, seat allocation, and deck space allocation on a departure-by-departure basis. The business rule engine must be pre-loaded with hundreds of carefully thought-out standard rules, which can be further configured and automated to integrate seamlessly with the booking system. Introducing enhanced functionalities, such as bulk or group travel bookings, travel agent bookings, integration with online gift shops, dynamic seat selection, vacation and accommodation bookings, activities booking, vacation packaging, support for multiple onboard restaurants or food selection, and numerous other enhancements showcased on our main website.

The rule engine also engages and governs the behaviour of the online reservation and ticketing systems, ensuring seamless integration with the booking and checking processes. It controls customer relationship management, providing a comprehensive view of each customer through a single customer profile and facilitating rewards programs and other related features.

Additionally, the system would incorporate integrated support for gift cards, vouchers, and incentive cards, along with compatibility for multiple payment gateways to accommodate evolving safety and security requirements. This integration is achieved while maintaining or even enhancing the overall customer experience.

With hundreds of standard rules already included and the ability to easily add configurable options, the future traveller-centric system offers countless solutions to meet various business requirements. The powerful 'Business Meta Rule Engine' then serves as the backbone of this system, enabling rapid implementation and customization, leading to a seamless and efficient experience for both customers and businesses.

Advantages of Rule Engines

Revenue management with configurable and editable rules adds a set of advantages to your applications:

1. Greater flexibility: keeping your rules in an internal business rule engine knowledge base let you adapt easily your decisions when they are changing.
2. Easier to grasp: Rules are easier to understand than procedural code so they can be effectively used to bridge the gap between business analysts and developers.
3. Reduced complexity: When embedding lots of decision points to your procedural codes it can easily turn your website application into a nightmare. IMS provides hundreds of rules as a standard to better handle increasing complexity because it uses a consistent representation of business rules.
4. Reusability: By keeping rules in one place it leads to greater reusability of business rules.

The flexible rules-based booking engine can be configured to support virtually any type of reservation. It comprises hundreds of editable and configurable rules as standard.

It should also provide variable-based templates which contain generic pre-defined rules based on the module or modules integrated.

Connecting the City with Mobile Ticketing Systems

Many of us are used to mobile ticketing software when it comes to buying train tickets or paying for subway fares, but the future of mobile ticketing technology spans a much wider scope than that.

Travellers will need to move through the smart cities of the future flawlessly, skipping lengthy queues for train tickets, purchasing subway travel on their phone, paying for cabs with mobile apps, scanning bus fares using their smartphones, renting bicycles with a mobile ticketing platform and even staying ahead of transport delays with online updates.

The cities of the future will begin to use Traveller-centric systems to their advantage, creating a seamless network of transport and information that can be accessed easily via a smartphone. These systems will be especially valuable in helping to address transportation challenges in urban areas (to reduce congestion caused by single-occupancy vehicles), transit deserts, and as a replacement for fixed routes during off-peak hours. These smart mobile ticketing solutions will alleviate everything from waiting times and queuing, to the need to carry cash and tickets, to being late for work because of a delay.

We all know one of the biggest pitfalls of travelling is the time it takes to travel. Most journeys require more than one method of transport. Take a holiday... You might be flying to one city, getting a train from the airport, and then taking a ferry to your final destination.

Travelling short distances isn't necessarily simpler either. We all know the score when it comes to journeying through a city. You might leave home and jump on a bus, fumbling for change to buy your ticket, from here you might need to board a train, queueing for your ticket at the station. From the train, you might need to enter a subway network, where you'll need a different type of ticket, and from your last stop on the subway, you might need to hail a cab or call an Uber to get to your final destination.

One journey can mean as many as four or five different transit methods, and these are usually all split between different ticketing solutions.

Most travellers are aware of the latest technology when it comes to ticketing, but this area is fast advancing, with mobile ticketing technology set to improve journeys of the future.

As more travel providers integrate mobile ticketing systems into their infrastructure, the transitions between these journeys are becoming ever easier. Now, as well as buying your transport on the internet via online ticketing technology, you can store all your travel cards and tickets on your smartphone with mobile ticketing software. This negates the need to queue for tickets, fumble for money and search for your travel card, making the transition between different types of transit far smoother than ever before.

Imagine a world where you can board every transport provider with just your smartphone or your smartwatch, paying for travel as you go, showing pre-booked tickets and getting updates about your journey to ensure you're taking the best route at the time.

As emerging mobility services such as bike-share, carshare, ride-sourcing, ride-sharing, and on-demand transit, coupled with trip planning, scheduling, transfer, and navigation platforms, are changing the way people get around. These new mobility services have important implications for public transportation, such as serving as first/last-mile solutions or shifting demand to other modes of mobility services, especially in urban areas and cities.

These are the journeys of the future, and they're far more comfortable thanks to Mobility on Demand digital platforms that help travellers plan their journey and package the various mode options, allowing them to choose whatever is most efficient for them — be it the shortest travel time, lowest cost, fewest transfers, or limited walking.

That is how an integrated public/private mobility system should meet the needs of individual travellers, be they, tourists or local citizens.

Traveller Expectations of Integrated and Seamless Mobility Options

The world is getting smarter. And with over half the global population now living in urban areas, we are seeing a change in the way we live in our cities. In the modern world, it is no longer enough to exist as a city, now we need to evolve into smart cities.

As smart city integration is introduced to tourist destinations across the world, these cities are connecting their resources online, generating real-time interaction between objects and the internet. Because of this, tourists can travel across these destinations while interacting with activities, attractions and events, navigating across the city easily, discovering fresh and unique sights, and continually passing this data back to the city and tourist companies, who can, in turn, provide tailored customer service.

Smart tourist destination software can enhance the tourist experience in many ways. For example, it can track the movement of visitors via a ticket chip at a gallery. This supplies information that can be used to provide better resources or marketing opportunities. Or it can observe the movement of guests at an event, providing real-time data that can be employed for refreshment opportunities, opening and closing entrances and exits, or managing traffic. Smart city software can even be utilized in providing mobile visitor tours, showing tourists the side of a city that they might not otherwise discover.

All the while the information provided via these implemented systems can help tourist boards and businesses better manage their resources and advertising, and overall provide an enhanced experience for visitors.

Blueprint for Tomorrow's Cities: The Evolution of Smart City Technology

It is estimated that by the year 2025, 80 per cent of the world's population will own a smartphone. This is changing the way we live and the way we move across our planet.

As the general public is becoming more accustomed to using their smartphones as part of everyday life, we are looking to integrate them into our business models, modernizing our services and giving our customers easy access to our resources via their smartphones. As travellers, we are more technologically aware, and this is reflected in the way our customers utilize their smartphones in booking travel, learning about routes and gaining real-time information.

From tourist operators to transport providers, smart passenger software is a crucial aspect of modern business. Online ticketing is now seen by many customers as standard, and many users have come to expect the ability to book their travel online and via their smartphones. By implementing smart passenger software into your business, you can better understand your customer's needs, you can plan your resources more appropriately, and you can cut down on costs and waiting times.

The future of account-based ticketing and payments in making major cities "smart cities" is the ability to provide a framework that allows multiple organizations to link their cards or apps into a single, seamless system.

For example, activity providers, major venues and transit operators can integrate to create combined access, travel and in-venue payment experience. This would allow smart cards, membership cards and other payment methods to be utilized across the city not only for transit but for entrance into venues, book activities, and purchase from retailers all able to link up to the same system and utilize the same access and payment system.

The shift to open payments for online booking, reservations, ticketing and payments, like every other major technological change, has its own unique set of challenges and complications. One of the first issues to be considered is whether customers in a specific regional market have sufficient adoption rates of contactless EMV payment cards and NFC devices to benefit from an open payment scheme

It is becoming increasingly clear, that the entire transit industry and smart city tourist ecosystems are part of a shift to enable more cost-efficient and easier ways for passengers to make reservations, issue tickets and also allow operators to process fare collections.

As well as providing an easy platform for customers to purchase and store travel tickets, smart passenger software can enhance your customers' travelling experience. As they move across your network, whether they are travelling on a train, by boat, or even on a plane, they can gain real-time information about the transport network. This allows you to better manage your network, whether it's in advising passengers of a different route if there has been a delay, or in giving them an estimated time of arrival.

The way the world is moving is changing, and smart passenger software will help you make the most of this exciting new world for your business.

Reservation & Ticketing Connections

There is much said regarding today's traveller. Such as today's travellers want to simply turn up and go. They want real-time information. Printed tickets are out and mobile ticketing using mobile technology is in.

Supposedly smart travel systems can do all this and make travel efficient and the experience more enjoyable.

At issue today is the fact that creating a technology ecosystem for transport providers and users must also take into account the reasons why people are travelling and their use of the latest technology, whilst retaining access to legacy systems.

Some are travelling for business, and as such you need fast and timely transportation. Others are travelling for pleasure and will require accommodation, activities, perhaps rental requirements and so many other necessary items to make their vacations a truly memorable experience.

Thus we start to see how the proliferation of information and communication technologies in the 21st century impacts society, business and people in everyday contexts in urban and resort destinations, particularly concerning tourism.

"Smart" has become an increasingly popular buzzword to describe technological, social and economic developments filled by smart technologies that rely on sensors, open data, APIs and new ways of connectivity between humans and machines. The mobile revolution, and specifically the role of the smartphone and supporting travel experiences certainly fit into this context.

The advent of so-called smart tourism, thus allows tourists to better communicate and interact within cities to establish closer relationships with residents, local businesses, activities, local government, city attractions and area transit and transportation.

Yet, smart tourism although is becoming increasingly prominent, has not been well documented, conceptualized or otherwise discussed, except on a fragmented basis and much exists on legacy platforms.

Cities and local governments in general, tend to run the local bus, train and other transit services. Depending upon the infrastructure inherent within the cities, one sees a range of ticketing options ranging from no tickets and cash payments, onboard ticketing, to online reservation with paper ticketing and barcode support to the more sophisticated cities with smart cards, mobile ticketing, etc.

Sitting aside from these transit infrastructures, cities have a wide range of personal transportation, taxes, limousine services and other ancillary transportation. The majority of the transit or transportation services do not in any way interact with local activities other than to provide pass-through or final mile services to reach those activity disembarkation points.

We must then also consider accommodation providers, such as hotels, bed-and-breakfast providers, shuttle companies, tour & activity providers, campgrounds and marinas.

So, although we see the local city government providing a certain level of smart connected transit options, we typically see little internal integration within a destination of its activity, accommodation, parking and other touristic requirements into a single "Smart" entity.

What we currently see, are large travel website organizations such as Priceline, Expedia and Booking.com, etc., providing packaged vacations to destinations. At the other end of the spectrum, we have the large destination companies such as Sandals and Atlantis, etc.

This leaves the single activity and transit operators to market their product websites to attract bookings and reservations.

As such, few of the reservation and ticketing systems in use today can integrate within a smart city environment.

Except, this is where a Traveller-centric system reservation and ticketing system comes into play.

Due to its many modules that cover the complete panoply of reservation and ticketing requirements for smart tourism destinations including a range of transit and transportation options, it will provide a complete smart ecosystem for tourism destination competitiveness.

A smart city destination marketing organization can establish itself with the appropriate connections and interactions with tourism operators, other governmental departments, and the data and develop an overall smart tourism strategy formulation at the city or even regional levels.

Implementation of activity and transit websites allows sister systems to communicate directly with each other's databases to share product information, and pricing with appropriate reservation and ticketing options, including interagency, inter-company commissioning and market pricing.

Apart from the integration of related activity, accommodation and transportation websites at a destination, we need to look at new and emerging technologies for airport access, train and bus stations and that goes for the arriving intercity traveller.

At the time of trip planning, the intercity traveller needs information about ground transportation options simultaneously with the selection of their airline trip. An intercity traveller, for example, may want ground connection information at their arrival destination. At present, the information available to the traveller about ground transportation services at the destination and of their trip is often sporadic and incomplete.

With a Traveller-centric system, you can establish an integrated range of local transportation services to not only disseminate ground transportation information to these arriving passengers but also provide total integration of bus reservation and ticketing options, routes and schedules to those travellers in a user-friendly format.

Innovation in Reservation and Fare Collection Technology

One of the many concerns of companies, not only in the business of passenger transportation but also the provision of tourism and activity destination providers is their legacy technology and integrating newer innovations in reservation and fare collection technology.

Typically, the predominant means of providing transit tickets and also for entry into activities and the boarding of tour buses has been by the means of old-fashioned paper tickets. To a certain extent, magnetic tickets and smart cards have been used depending on market circumstances.

Investment has been made within the required infrastructure to facilitate that payment and validate the tickets, as well as the means of printing and distributing the appropriate ticket formats.

As seen, over the last few years, the provision of paper tickets in more advanced regions of the world has seen a decline of paper tickets, offset by an increase in the use of the smartphone and contactless cards, or now more frequently called mobile ticketing.

The majority of mobile ticketing is generally being implemented and available to larger agencies and operators due to their fairly large existing staff and technical expertise. They are generally able to deploy mobile ticketing to run alongside their existing fare collection system, by deploying visual digital ticket inspection by drivers alongside their existing paper ticket scam solutions.

But, primarily operators of mass transit drive these solutions. It is a requirement suitable for the purchase of a ticket, and use that ticket as part of an unreserved seat on some form of a vehicle.

This may be suitable for operators of mass transit but is not always suitable in the tourism industry, whereby tourists wish to identify a particular time and seat availability for their travel purposes.

The fact is that even though mobile barcode and QR code are becoming the most accepted way to deliver contactless mobile ticketing in larger passenger transportation operations, it is not always applicable to many in the tourism industry.

This breaks the reservation and ticketing industry into two major parts. At one end we have the airline and railway industry, plus large ferry-type operations.

These typically use older legacy systems due to the more complex requirements for their reservation and ticketing processes. At the other end of the scale, we have the more up-to-date mobile fare collection technologies coming into play.

Both of these approaches are expensive and tend to be out of reach for the majority of smaller to medium-sized operators within the tourism industry, both for some form of passenger transportation and the provision of tourism activities and accommodation, etc.

But, there is a third option. And of course, we are talking about a Traveller-centric system.

It not only allows you to implement all of the capabilities of a front-line airline and ferry reservation and ticketing system but also allows you to also implement the full capabilities of mobile ticketing for a fraction of the cost.

Saving the planet or just saving some space in your wallet, online ticketing and mobile ticketing are both increasingly popular choices when it comes to buying travel, events tickets and even tickets to tourist attractions.

As mobile ticket transaction becomes more and more prevalent, are we about to see the death of the paper ticket?

Customers Prefer Online Ticketing

Transit operators have predicted a shift in their ticketing payment systems over the next five years. According to a recent survey, although around 50% of customers still report using paper tickets at the moment, just 14% of them thought they would still be using paper tickets in five years. As the world is getting to grips with smart technology, they are certainly looking to exploit it more for their everyday activities and transactions.

Companies have also reported that they find online ticketing and mobile ticketing a lot more straightforward, particularly when it comes to selling transportation. A recent survey suggested that almost 50% of transit agencies find that handling cash is a hindrance and that their passengers also have concerns when it comes to paying with cash. Mobile and online ticketing solutions are changing the landscape of this business, and it is set to do so more and more in future.

Although this area of the market is still fairly new, an increasing number of people are turning to contactless and mobile technologies to pay for their tickets. Companies are expanding into this area rapidly, and customers have often been quick to respond, utilizing the technology they have to make their journeys and ticketing transactions even easier. Mobile barcodes, mobile NFC and contactless EMV services are expected to become more widespread over the next few years, and this spells the end of the paper ticket.

Tourism Reservation & Ticketing Software

As previously mentioned, "Smart" has become a new buzzword to describe technological, economic and social developments fueled by technologies that rely on sensors, big data, open data, new ways of connectivity and the exchange of information.

Smart tourism is also a new buzzword applied to describe the increasing reliance of tourism destinations, their industries and their tourists on emerging forms of IoT that allow for massive amounts of data to be transformed into value propositions.

In the context of tourism, smart technologies are changing consumer experiences and generating creative tourism business models. Cloud computing, big data, mobile apps, location-based services, virtual reality, augmented reality, and SNSs are all cutting-edge examples of smart technologies enhancing tourism experiences and services.

It is not so much the individual technological advances but rather the interconnection, synchronization and concerted use of different technologies that constitute smartness. As such, we are beginning to see a paradigm shift in the way travel and tourism are dealt with in a smart city environment.

Currently, the general tourist market relies on a multitude of different company websites, each with its version of reservation software suitable at the basic level of being able to confirm reservations for tours, travel, activities, events, etc.

In parallel, there also exist websites and travel sites listing accommodation and tourism packages for particular destinations. Also, existing within a destination you have a variety of mechanisms to produce transit tickets for collections, shuttle services, taxes, bicycle rentals, ride share and a host of other transport applications.

Within smart cities, a vast array of data services is being offered by open-source APIs to be utilized by third-party developers typically feeding mobile applications.

So, we have hundreds of tourist, transit and data touchpoints, yet most remain completely separate from each other.

Enter Artificial Intelligence (AI)

Artificial intelligence (AI) is transforming the way we live, work, and travel. AI can be integrated into a smart city tourist and transit system and benefits both visitors and residents.

AI can enhance the visitor experience by providing personalized recommendations, information, and assistance. For example, AI-powered intelligent chatbots can become reliable city assistants. Integrated with smart tourism apps, intelligent chatbots can manage flights and bookings, provide translation services, and deliver all the necessary information about city services, tourist attractions, events, restaurants, and more.

AI can also drive economic growth and sustainability by supporting smart tourism destination planning and development. For example, AI can help destinations analyze visitor behaviour, preferences, and feedback to design better products and services. AI can also help destinations monitor environmental impacts and implement strategies to reduce carbon footprint and waste.

In conclusion, AI is a powerful tool that can help smart cities create a better tourist and transit system. By integrating AI into various aspects of city life, smart cities can offer a more enjoyable, efficient, and eco-friendly experience to their visitors and residents.

The Traveller-centric smart city software approach using Ai is to take an inclusive view, implementing a user-orientated integrated design of all system touch points and interfaces with the customer.

Traveller-centric Ai allows the creation of a multi-modal information, booking and payment system, linking individual activity, events, rental, ride-share, parking and hoteliers with those of public and private transport.

Traveller-centric Ai plus smart city software APIs can enable passenger transport companies to create multimodal services, which exactly meet the needs of the next generation of urban dwellers.

Traveller-centric reservation & ticketing software can be used on individual websites or scaled up to be used in the creation of a Smart City digital market that can include multiple tenants, multiple websites, open datasets and data from paid sources, where data services from different partners and vendors can be exposed, priced, monetized and consumed from within a single platform.

It is also possible to improve direct people-to-people sales with Traveller-centric Ai and API features, designed for property owners, tour companies, Transit/Transport operators, online marketing companies, groups or chains by enabling their vendors to distribute rates and inventory online and become part of a significant and powerful sales, booking, ticketing and reservation "Smart City" e-distribution centre.

Acting as a centralized platform, such a system can re-master smart city data, tourism data, and third-party website data and package it for access to users via different channels, whether that's websites, kiosks, mobile devices and intelligent beacons.

This would include also a wide range of capabilities to take reservations for transit and produce tickets across a broad range of tourism activities and transit requirements.

It's the ability to also provide fully integrated capabilities to track public transportation in real-time and use geo-location to provide multiple options for reservations, itineraries, packages, accommodation, rentals, parking access, ride share companies and events in a fully homogenized manner can form the backbone of a smart city, smart tourism and destination system.

Tourism Platforms for Smart Cities

A purpose-built Traveller-centric system can be used on individual websites or scaled up to be used in the creation of a Smart City digital marketplace that can include multiple websites, open datasets and data from paid sources, where data services from different partners and vendors can be exposed, priced, monetized and consumed from within a single platform.

This can become a singular "Smart City" platform through the integration of electronic ticketing systems, transit reservations, fare collection, mapping & reservation capabilities for scenic spots, vehicle parking system, tour guide management system of travel agents, accommodation booking, rental reservations, digital room service and operation management system of hotels, last mile conveyance booking and function as a complete destination marketing system.

Using this system as a central travel, transit and tourism platform for smart cities can satisfy the individualized needs of city inhabitants, and tourists, and improve tourist satisfaction and the urban tourism function. Integrated systems facilitate Smart Tourism activities and provide specialized functionalities designed to offer services for Smart Communities, by using open standards and protocols, making data accessible, and adapting existing solutions to their needs.

This is what I would call a Smart Tourism Platform for a "Smart City": an area where government and private companies work together to provide the best cultural and entertainment services for tourists.

Museums, cultural associations, tourist attractions, activity providers, shuttle service companies, transit providers, but also hotels, bars and restaurants, cooperate not only in making their products, inventories and stories available for all tourists, but also in promoting them through one unique online platform.

Whenever new tourists arrive in a smart city, they can choose from a significant number of cultural and lifestyle outdoor and indoor tours.

They do not need to download a different app for every attraction they visit, on the contrary, they can rely on one trusted online guide to experience the city and its cultural attractions, as well as its shopping areas, restaurants, boat, cars, taxi and bike rental services, etc.

This implies that tourists are not the only ones enjoying a "smart city". The use of one platform to promote the city's cultural and lifestyle attractions is a great plus for all the players operating within the tourism field because it can virtually bring new visitors to those sites that are usually less promoted. This can be done, for instance, by adding museums, churches and indoor points of interest to outdoor city tours. A smart city has many more ways to promote itself, online, offline and directly onsite by every attraction or tourist facility.

It is projected that by the year 2050, around 70% of the world will be living in a city or urban environment. With the world growing at such a rapid rate, our technology is as important as ever when it comes to keeping these cities moving, and that is why a new breed of the city is on the horizon...

Whether it's in enhancing public transport, improving access to facilities or just managing the day-to-day running of a city, technology now plays a huge part in the operations of any urban environment.

Enhancing Mobility: Unraveling Transit Travellers and Cargo Transport

The development of a smart city reservation and ticketing software application for ancillary transportation connections is crucial in meeting the diverse functional designs within the ferry, bus, and water taxi industries. This application needs to be modular and highly configurable, allowing operators to tailor it to their specific needs.

The primary goal of this integrated Traveller-centric System is to provide a seamless experience for travellers, enabling them to reserve transit paths conveniently from any workplace or online platform. Furthermore, it should offer comprehensive visibility of all reservations to management, ensuring efficient operations and effective resource allocation.

To accommodate the various fare structures prevalent in the industry, the application must support a complete range of pricing options. This includes concessions for eligible individuals, such as seniors or students, as well as different fare categories for children and adults. Moreover, the system should allow for group bookings and the purchase of multiple journey tickets, providing flexibility to meet the diverse needs of travellers.

In addition to standard fare rates, the software application should incorporate Intelligent Pricing capabilities. This feature enables users to enter special deals and non-standard fare rates, allowing operators to offer dynamic pricing based on factors such as demand, time of day, or special events. This functionality enhances revenue management and helps optimize pricing strategies to maximize profitability.

Such as systems that can handle a whole range of airline-style pricing. This allows customers to not only pay the full applicable fare in advance, without paying a separate reservation fee, receive tickets and boarding passes online and also have access to a full range of discounted fares subject to availability.

Another essential aspect of the application is its ability to manage commission percentages for travel agents and account holders. By allowing operators to set commission rates, the software enables the determination of discounts for these entities. This feature encourages collaboration with travel agents and facilitates loyalty programs for account holders, creating a mutually beneficial ecosystem.

I would summarise by stating that, the smart city reservation and ticketing software application should be modular, highly configurable, and cater to the functional designs of the ferry, bus, and water taxi operators. It should provide a traveller-centric experience, allowing reservations from any workplace and online platform, while also offering comprehensive visibility to management. The application must support a wide range of fare structures, including concessions, children, adults, group bookings, and multiple journey tickets. Furthermore, it should incorporate Intelligent Pricing capabilities, allowing users to input special deals and non-standard fare rates. Lastly, the software should enable the management of commission percentages, enabling the determination of discounts for travel agents and account holders.

Multi-Tenant Traveller-centric Ferry & Bus Support

To streamline the procedure of arranging, building, and maintaining a multi-tenant Ferry and Bus Network Reservation and ticketing abilities or multi-channel booking company model for a smart city, there is a need to develop a comprehensive solution that actively facilitates cooperation between resellers, suppliers, and consumers. The development to create a total reservation and merchandising system goes beyond the standard booking and payment procedure, by incorporating all the necessary components for effective online selling and marketing, with centralized management from a single back-end administration.

One of the key aspects of this development is the creation of an application that enables online credit card payments, deposits, and timely payments through a selected payment gateway. This ensures a seamless and secure payment process for customers. Additionally, the system should have the capability to incorporate other ferryboat or bus lines, allowing for expanded services and increased options for customers.

A calendar-driven booking feature is crucial to efficiently managing reservations. This feature would provide a user-friendly interface for customers to select their desired travel dates and routes, while also ensuring that the available inventory is accurately reflected. The system should be able to handle multiple bookings simultaneously, avoiding conflicts and double bookings.

Detailed client data reports are an essential part of this development. The system should capture and store relevant customer information, such as contact details, travel preferences, and booking history. These data reports would enable the company to better understand customer behaviour, tailor marketing strategies, and provide personalized services. The reports should be easily accessible and offer comprehensive insights into customer trends and patterns.

Transit & Tour Freight Handling Features

In addition to the primary reservation and ticketing system for passengers, it is important to consider incorporating the ability to handle freight and other cargo. This feature would allow sales agents and administrators to establish a freight operation, making efficient use of any available cargo capacity on various modes of transportation such as buses, ferries, and even aircraft.

To accommodate this functionality, it is necessary to integrate dynamic selectable digital floor or space maps. These maps would enable the visualization and allocation of cargo space within the vehicles. By utilizing such technology, sales agents and administrators can easily identify and assign appropriate areas for carrying freight, optimizing the utilization of the available space.

Moreover, this freight handling capability should seamlessly integrate with the envisioned end-to-end delivery and transportation options of the smart city Traveller-centric system. This ensures a holistic approach to transportation, where passenger and cargo services are integrated and coordinated efficiently, contributing to an overall smarter and more sustainable urban mobility ecosystem.

Considerations for the design of this feature include:

1. Scalability: The system should be designed to handle varying amounts of freight demand, accommodating different types and sizes of cargo.
2. Flexibility: The design should allow for easy customization and adaptation to different modes of transportation, ensuring compatibility with buses, ferries, and aircraft.
3. User-friendly interface: Sales agents and administrators should have intuitive tools to set up and manage the freight operation. The interface should provide clear visual representations of cargo capacity and allow for easy allocation and tracking of shipments.
4. Integration with existing systems: The freight handling capability should seamlessly integrate with the main reservation and ticketing system, ensuring a unified and cohesive user experience.
5. Real-time updates: The system should provide real-time information on available cargo capacity and the status of ongoing shipments, allowing sales agents and administrators to make informed decisions and optimize resource allocation.
6. Security and privacy: Adequate measures should be implemented to protect the privacy and security of freight-related data and ensure the safe handling of valuable or

sensitive cargo.

7. Interoperability: The design should consider interoperability standards to enable collaboration with external logistics providers, facilitating seamless end-to-end transportation solutions.

By carefully addressing these design considerations, the integration of freight handling capabilities within the reservation and ticketing system can enhance the efficiency and effectiveness of transportation services, supporting the overall objectives of the smart city Traveller-centric system.

Mail & Package Shipping

In the context of freight operations, an additional aspect to be taken into account is the inclusion of mail and packages as a means of enhancing smart city revenues. This can be achieved either by incorporating them into the existing system or by integrating them with other delivery Application Programming Interfaces (APIs).

Several design considerations need to be addressed to ensure the efficient implementation of this functionality. Firstly, the administrator should have the capability to add a comprehensive list of locations that will serve as the origin and destination points for the mail and packages. This ensures that the system can accurately determine the pickup and delivery locations based on user requests.

Moreover, the administrator should be able to specify a separate list of pick-up locations specifically designated for the main locations mentioned earlier. This enables the system to streamline the process and facilitate efficient retrieval of mail and packages from these specific points.

In addition, shipping costs should be treated as distinct products with unique parameters. The administrator should have the ability to add these costs to the system, ensuring that they are accurately reflected during the shipping process. By defining specific parameters for shipping costs, such as weight, dimensions, or delivery speed, the system can provide accurate and transparent pricing information to the users.

Expanding on the design considerations, integration with other delivery APIs becomes essential. By connecting with external delivery services, the system can leverage its existing infrastructure and resources to handle mail and package shipments. This integration allows for broader reach and potentially increases revenue streams for the smart city. Seamless integration with delivery APIs requires careful planning and coordination to ensure compatibility and smooth data exchange between systems.

Overall, the design considerations for incorporating mail and packages into the freight operations of a smart city involve enabling the administrator to manage origin/destination locations, specifying pick-up locations, defining shipping costs as distinct products with relevant parameters, and facilitating integration with other delivery APIs. These considerations aim to optimize efficiency, accuracy, and revenue generation within the smart city ecosystem.

Charter Reservation Software

To enhance the functionality of the Traveller-centric system, it would be recommended to design and integrate a comprehensive charter inquiry and booking engine as part of the smart city infrastructure. Such a feature would enable operators to efficiently manage online inquiries and streamline the process of booking charters, thereby maximizing their potential revenue.

The integrated charter booking feature will serve as a centralized platform for operators to handle charter inquiries and bookings. Through this feature, operators can effectively manage the entire process, from initial inquiry to final confirmation. The system will provide operators with the necessary tools to respond to inquiries promptly and provide customized responses based on the specific requirements of potential charter clients.

To facilitate the booking process, the system should incorporate an offer generation system. This feature will simplify the creation and sending of offers to potential charter clients. Operators can input the relevant details, such as tour times, departure options, and rental periods, and the system will automatically generate customized offers based on this information. By automating this process, operators can save valuable time and increase their efficiency in converting inquiries into successful bookings.

A key aspect of a traveller-centric system is real-time inventory control. This functionality will be extended to both regular departure seating and charter bookings. By implementing real-time inventory control, operators can efficiently manage and allocate their available resources, ensuring optimal utilization of vehicles, equipment, and personnel. This also enables operators to provide travellers with accurate and up-to-date information regarding seat availability and charter options, enhancing their overall experience.

In addition to inventory control, the system should incorporate advanced scheduling capabilities. This includes the ability to manage and optimize the allocation of resources based on demand, traffic conditions, and other factors. Operators can leverage data analytics and predictive algorithms to dynamically adjust schedules, ensuring that resources are efficiently deployed and travellers' needs are met effectively.

To further enhance the system's functionality, integration with other smart city components should be considered. For example, integrating with real-time traffic data can enable operators to anticipate potential delays and adjust schedules accordingly, minimizing disruptions and improving overall service reliability. Integration with payment gateways and accounting systems can streamline the financial aspects of charter bookings, allowing for seamless transactions and accurate record-keeping.

Overall, the integration of a fully integrated charter inquiry and booking engine within the smart city system will significantly benefit operators and travellers alike. By automating and streamlining the charter booking process, operators can save time, increase conversion rates, and provide a personalized experience for potential charter clients. Meanwhile, travellers will benefit from real-time inventory control, efficient resource management, and a seamless booking process, ultimately leading to an enhanced travel experience within the smart city environment.

From Paper to Pixels: The Evolution of Ticketing in the Mobile Era

Mobile ticketing has emerged as one of the most convenient and user-friendly methods for customers to purchase tickets for various modes of transportation. With the advancement of technology, mobile ticketing has revolutionized the ticketing experience by providing passengers with the ability to buy tickets anytime and anywhere, at their complete convenience.

Beyond serving as a ticket-purchasing platform, smartphones offer a multitude of features that enhance the overall travel experience for passengers. In addition to buying tickets, travellers can conveniently store their tickets directly on their mobile devices, eliminating the need for physical copies. Furthermore, mobile ticketing apps provide a platform for passengers to seek information, ask questions, and receive real-time updates about their journey. By harnessing the power of smartphones, transport operators can integrate a smart and innovative system within their network, enhancing the overall customer experience.

When considering a ticketing software update, the mobile ticketing platform presents itself as one of the easiest and most cost-effective options to implement. It requires minimal installation time and resources compared to contactless or smart-card systems. Moreover, mobile ticketing software can be easily updated or expanded upon in the future, providing the flexibility to transition to a contactless approach if desired. It is worth noting that mobile ticketing software can be seamlessly integrated with passengers' preferred ticketing methods, catering to a wide range of preferences and not solely limited to mobile ticketing sales.

Implementing mobile ticketing systems does not restrict passengers to exclusively using mobile ticketing software. On the contrary, it empowers them to choose the ticket purchase and travel method that best suits their needs, whether it be the convenience of mobile tickets or the familiarity of traditional paper tickets. This flexibility enhances customer satisfaction by accommodating their preferences and ensuring a seamless ticketing experience.

In summary, mobile ticketing has emerged as an incredibly convenient and versatile solution for ticket purchases in the transportation industry. By leveraging the power of smartphones, transport operators can provide passengers with a comprehensive range of features, from purchasing and storing tickets to receiving real-time updates. Updating ticketing software to include a mobile ticketing platform is a cost-effective and flexible option that allows for future scalability and integration with passengers' preferred ticketing methods. Ultimately, embracing mobile ticketing empowers passengers to choose the ticketing and travel options that best suit their individual needs and preferences.

Connected Journeys

We all know one of the biggest pitfalls of travelling is the time it takes to travel. Most journeys require more than one method of transport. Take a holiday... You might be flying to one city, getting a train from the airport, and then taking a ferry to your final destination.

Travelling short distances isn't necessarily simpler either. We all know the score when it comes to journeying through a city. You might leave home and jump on a bus, fumbling for change to buy your ticket, from here you might need to board a train, queueing for your ticket at the station. From the train, you might need to enter a subway network, where you'll need a different type of ticket, and from your last stop on the subway, you might need to hail a cab to get to your final destination.

One journey can mean as many as four or five different transit methods, and these are usually all split between different ticketing solutions.

Door-to-Door Transit Application Systems

Most travellers are aware of the latest technology when it comes to ticketing, but this area is fast advancing, with mobile ticketing technology set to improve journeys of the future.

As more travel providers integrate mobile ticketing systems into their infrastructure, the transitions between these journeys are becoming ever easier. Now, as well as buying your transport on the internet via online ticketing technology, you can store all your travel cards and tickets on your smartphone with mobile ticketing software. This negates the need to queue for tickets, fumble for money and search for your travel card, making the transition between different types of transit far smoother than ever before.

Imagine a world where you can board every transport provider with just your smartphone or your smartwatch, paying for travel as you go, showing pre-booked tickets and getting updates about your journey to ensure you're taking the best route at the time.

These are the journeys of the future, and they're far more comfortable thanks to mobile ticketing solutions.

Smart City Websites, Interoperability and Mobility

The world is starting to travel smarter. Cities are beginning to implement modern technology so their residents can live easier lives and move freely around the urban metropolis, and this is something that can also benefit tourists. The lines between the psychical and the digital are blurring and with this, we welcome a new era of travel and tourism.

Urban areas are now looking for new ways of improving their visitor experience, and this is seeing the rise of smart tourism. Using the techniques and procedures in place to create these so-called smart cities, these areas are now looking to extend their technology to tourists, supporting tourism with a fresh and modern approach.

As smart cities are emerging across the globe, those who are taking it further are developing into smart destinations, keeping their visitors in mind as well as their residents when developing their technological infrastructures. To maintain mobility, resources and sustainability, these cities and even some rural areas are looking to the quality of the day-to-day lives of their residents as well as their visitors.

The Smart Tourism Destinations concept emerges from the development of Smart Cities bringing smartness into tourism destinations. This requires dynamically interconnecting stakeholders through a technological platform on which information relating to tourism activities could be exchanged instantly.

Such an integrated platform would require multiple touchpoints that could be accessed through a variety of end-user devices that would support the creation and facilitation of real-time tourism experiences and improve the effectiveness of tourism resource management throughout the destination.

Smart Destinations Software

Smart city software is now being implemented across the world. Urban areas are constantly looking for information and communication technology to bring their areas into the modern age and smart tourist destinations software is looking to take this one step further. With smart city integration, we can now expect smart cities to do more, whether it's in communicating tourist information to visitors via a mobile app, giving them a mobile ticketing service that allows them to book transport across the city they are visiting, or translating tourist signs for those who don't speak the local language.

The world is evolving and becoming more and more connected by the day, and the development and use of smart tourist destinations software will ensure you are leading the movement and promoting a better way for people to explore the world.

Traveller-centric software provides such a framework for smart tourism destinations, towards enhancing their destinations' competitiveness.

The Traveller-centric system development for a Smart City also facilitates seamless access to value-added services both for its citizens and tourists as city visitors, such as access to real-time reservations to venues, and activities and access to the destinations' private and public transportation networks.

Successful destinations can be structured to show attractions, accessibility and services facilitating a convenient day, namely accommodation, gastronomy and leisure activities also available packages and services are bundled by intermediaries to direct tourists' attention to certain unique features of that destination.

Traveller-centric software combining modular digital ecosystems and smart business API networks as conceptual building blocks, further provides conceptualizations utilizing smart technologies, allowing smart tourism destinations to envision new ways in which value is created exchanged and consumed at that destination.

It provides the software technology to introduce new destination business models and interaction paradigms that can be easily scaled for local, entity-specific implementations, or large-scale regional Smart City tourism destination applications.

Revolutionizing Reservation Systems: A Closer Look at Traveller-Centric Software

Traveller-centric reservation software for a smart city should be designed to enhance the overall travel experience of individuals by integrating various aspects such as tourism, accommodation, transit, parking, e-commerce, and end-to-end mobility. Here's an overview of what such a software solution could comprise:

1. User-Friendly Interface: The reservation software should have an intuitive and user-friendly interface that allows travellers to easily navigate and access various services.

2. Tourism Information: The software should provide comprehensive information about the city's tourist attractions, including landmarks, historical sites, cultural events, and local experiences. This can include interactive maps, virtual tours, and multimedia content to assist travellers in planning their itineraries.

3. Accommodation Booking: Integration with hotels, guesthouses, and vacation rentals should be provided to enable travellers to search, compare, and book accommodations based on their preferences, budget, and availability. The software can offer detailed descriptions, photos, reviews, and ratings for each property.

4. Transit Services: The software should integrate with the city's public transportation systems, including buses, trains, trams, and taxis, providing real-time schedules, routes, and fare information. It can also offer ticket purchasing options, including mobile ticketing and contactless payment methods.

5. Parking Management: To address parking concerns, the

software can provide real-time availability and reservation of parking spots, guiding travellers to vacant spaces and minimizing the time spent searching for parking. Integration with smart parking systems and payment platforms can streamline the process.

6. E-commerce Integration: Travelers can benefit from an integrated e-commerce platform within the software, allowing them to explore and purchase local products, souvenirs, event tickets, and services offered by local businesses. This can foster economic growth and support the local community.

7. End-to-End Mobility Solutions: The software should facilitate seamless interconnectivity between different modes of transportation, enabling travellers to plan multi-modal journeys. It can provide personalized travel recommendations, including optimal routes, transfers, and estimated travel times.

8. Personalization and Recommendations: By leveraging user preferences, travel history, and data analytics, the software can offer personalized recommendations for attractions, accommodations, transportation, and experiences, enhancing the overall travel experience.

9. Multi-Language and Accessibility: To cater to a diverse range of travellers, the software should support multiple languages and accessibility features, ensuring inclusivity and ease of use for all users.

10. Integration with Smart City Infrastructure: The reservation software can integrate with other smart city systems, such as traffic management, environmental sensors, and emergency services, to provide real-time updates and enhance safety and efficiency for travellers.

11. Feedback and Reviews: The software should allow travellers

to provide feedback, ratings, and reviews for accommodations, transportation services, and tourism experiences. This helps improve the quality of services and provides valuable insights to other travellers.

12. Mobile App and Notifications: Offering a mobile application with push notifications can enhance the traveller's convenience and engagement by providing timely updates, alerts, and reminders.

By incorporating these features and functionalities, traveller-centric reservation software can streamline the travel experience within a smart city, making it more efficient, enjoyable, and convenient for both residents and visitors.

Tour Reservation Software

Not all tour reservation software is created equally. While the majority of tour reservation software systems available in the market today offer similar capabilities and performance, some differences may surprise you. These software systems are primarily offered as software-as-a-service (SaaS) and are typically evaluated based on their monthly cost and the basic requirements of tour reservation companies.

The key factors that differentiate tour reservation software include their user interface, workflow, and monthly rental costs associated with using them. Most of these software systems perform well and provide the necessary operational capabilities for small tour or activity companies. They are designed to meet the common needs of reservation websites in this industry.

However, if you require a more specialized or customized solution beyond the generic tour reservation software, your options become limited. Developing a turn-key system that meets your specific requirements would require significant time and financial investment.

In the context of a smart city environment, where multiple interconnected reservation and ticketing websites are needed, city-specific tour reservation software is necessary. Such a system would be installed directly on the city's domain web server, providing full control and ownership of customer data. It would also need to support a wide range of features, pricing, inventory configurations, and hundreds of configurable pre-set rules that are not typically available in single-user, single-site systems.

To cater to a large traveller-centric smart city environment, the tour reservation software should not only handle tour reservations but also accommodate rental services, accommodation bookings, campground reservations, marina services, e-commerce products, shuttle operations, and ferry, bus, and air operations. It should support trip reservations, ticketing, scheduling, and reservations made by visitors, as well as those made through travel representatives and corporate clients.

This comprehensive tour reservation software would be designed to meet the needs of various industries, such as adventure companies, boat reservations, cruise operators, coaches, shuttle services, zipline operators, dive centres, rafting companies, and many other tour and activity companies. Additionally, it would include integrated barcodes, QR codes, or wearable ticketing options to streamline the ticketing process. By delivering tickets and maintaining control over client relationships, brands, and profits, this software eliminates the need to pay continuous commissions.

In summary, while most tour reservation software systems are comparable in terms of basic capabilities and performance, there are specialized solutions available for specific needs. A comprehensive tour reservation software that caters to a smart city environment and supports various industries and reservation types can provide advanced features and greater control over operations, customer data, and profitability.

Reservation Software – Inventory Control

One of the fundamental aspects that determine the capabilities of a tour reservation system lies in its specialized inventory management system. The ease and effectiveness with which the tour reservation software enables users to create, price, allocate, and modify inventory in real-time serve as a true measure of the software's integrated real-time inventory management capabilities.

For instance, within a larger system, a tour reservation component should possess the ability to create inventory based on various parameters such as date, time, day, price, and period, allowing users to plan for up to two years in the future. Additionally, the software should also accommodate freight units, as having a tour reservation system capable of handling freight, mail, and mail packages as an ancillary option offers distinct advantages.

Furthermore, the system should enable users to override existing inventory based on seats, price, and freight units, either for specific time slots or for all times on a selected date. Alternatively, users should have the option to use a common inventory and allocate different numbers of available seats for each item, with the ability to select the option of "separate inventory for each tour/transit item."

Another advantageous feature would be the capability to clone inventory, which allows users to copy complex inventory periods, saving time and effort in setting up new inventory structures.

In addition to managing basic inventory, the software should provide the ability to work with fixed options and generate special options with or without associated inventory control. These options can be included or made optional, with or without a price, and should seamlessly integrate with the real-time inventory system.

Flexibility in adapting inventory rules is crucial, and the software should allow for changes such as setting maximum booking limits for tours. It should also enable the application of additional costs or discounts based on the number of hours before a tour takes place. Furthermore, the system should facilitate the establishment of entry limits based on the time before the trip or the maximum number of seats available for specified dates or times, enabling a timed release of seat allocations to the general public.

To cater to tours with varying seating arrangements, the software could incorporate dynamic seat maps for tour buses or other setups that require seat or table selection. Different seat maps can be linked to different periods and equipment, utilizing separate seat map files with distinct layouts for each specific period.

If a tour becomes unavailable, it would be advantageous to have the capability to swiftly transfer both the tour and its associated inventory and passengers to another time or date. The system should automatically accept existing reservations and provide updated barcoded tickets for the new time, ensuring a smooth transition for customers.

Additionally, it would be beneficial for the software to support packaged tours that include accommodations, flights, and other related services, providing a comprehensive solution for tour operators and customers alike.

RV Campground Boats & Marinas Reservations

By implementing minimal modifications to the existing Tour system, it can be effectively extended to handle RV Campground Boats & Marinas Reservations seamlessly. This enhancement introduces a comprehensive feature set, including a dynamic graphical map for campsite selection, enabling customers to conveniently reserve their desired site(s), and streamlining the payment process for a hassle-free reservation experience.

The incorporation of RV Campground Boats & Marinas Reservations into the existing system opens up a range of possibilities. The system can now cater to customers seeking reservations at various campgrounds, RV parks, and marinas, providing them with a unified platform to manage their bookings.

One of the prominent features of this enhanced system is the dynamic graphical map for campsite selection. Customers can visually explore available sites, view their amenities and surroundings, and choose the perfect spot for their RV or boat. The interactive map empowers users with an intuitive interface, allowing them to effortlessly browse through different locations, zoom in/out, and obtain detailed information about each site.

When customers have selected their preferred site(s), the system guides them through a straightforward reservation process. Users can enter their payment information securely and efficiently, with the assurance that their sensitive details are protected. The streamlined reservation process ensures that customers can complete their bookings with ease, saving them valuable time and effort.

Moreover, this enhanced system also facilitates management on the backend. Campground, RV park, and marina administrators gain access to an advanced dashboard that offers comprehensive tools for overseeing reservations, availability, and customer data. This allows administrators to efficiently manage the allocation of sites, handle cancellations or modifications, and generate reports for analysis and planning.

In summary, the extended Tour system now seamlessly accommodates RV Campground Boats & Marinas Reservations, delivering an enhanced experience for both customers and administrators. The addition of a dynamic graphical map for campsite selection, combined with a user-friendly and secure reservation process, makes it easier than ever for customers to reserve their desired sites. Meanwhile, administrators can effectively manage reservations and gain valuable insights through the advanced backend dashboard. This expansion broadens the system's scope and functionality, catering to the diverse needs of those seeking memorable outdoor experiences.

Hotel Reservation Software

To create a comprehensive and traveller-centric smart city system, it is crucial to explore partnerships with system property and hotel groups or chains. These collaborations would enable each property within these groups to effectively distribute room rates and inventory online, transforming them into integral components of a robust and influential hotel room booking and reservation e-distribution centre.

While there are already numerous established online accommodation providers, a truly smart city system should consider forming API-based partnerships with existing providers or even operating as an additional provider itself. By doing so, the system can offer end-to-end tourism services within a single transaction, streamlining the entire process for travellers.

One of the key features such a system can provide is a centralized platform for property and hotel chains to showcase their room rates and inventory online. This web-based central reservation system would allow guests to access available inventory across all properties in a convenient and consolidated manner. By centralizing this information, the booking process becomes significantly more efficient and less time-consuming for both guests and property/hotel owners.

In addition to the benefits mentioned above, when combined with other suggestions in this book, the smart city system can empower hotels to enhance their websites by offering direct and secure connections to travel agents and corporate clients, hotels can provide them with access to confidential rates and allotments. Moreover, internet users can enjoy the convenience of instant reservation confirmation of not only accommodation but local tours, transit, parking and other services in a single transaction, enhancing their booking experience.

Overall, a traveller-centric smart city system should establish partnerships with system property and hotel groups or chains. By creating a web-based central reservation system and integrating with existing providers or acting as an additional provider, the system can offer complete end-to-end tourism services.

Online Restaurant Reservation & Delivery

In the development of a smart city, it is crucial to consider the provision of reservation and ordering capabilities specifically tailored to the food industry. This aspect can be achieved through seamless integration with existing systems or as an additional feature within the city's comprehensive traveller-centric platform.

By incorporating reservation and ordering functionalities, the smart city can empower the food industry to streamline their operations, enhance customer experience, and maximize their potential in the digital age. Restaurants, cafes, and other food establishments can leverage these capabilities to enable customers to make reservations for dining, book private events, or even pre-order meals for pickup or delivery.

Integrating these features within the smart city's traveller-centric system offers a myriad of advantages. Firstly, it allows visitors and residents to conveniently access a wide range of food options, browse menus, and make reservations or orders through a centralized platform. This centralized approach enhances user convenience, as individuals can plan their dining experiences or place food orders without the need to navigate multiple independent applications.

Moreover, the food industry can tap into the integrated transit and tourist functions provided by the smart city system. This integration enables restaurants and eateries to capitalize on the influx of tourists and commuters by offering tailored promotions, such as special discounts or exclusive deals for individuals using specific transportation services or visiting popular attractions within the city. By aligning their offerings with the broader city ecosystem, the food industry can attract a larger customer base and foster positive customer engagement.

Additionally, the smart city's marketing functions serve as a valuable asset for the food industry. The system can incorporate an "upsell" facility, wherein restaurants can suggest additional menu items, upgrades, or complementary dishes to customers during the ordering process, thus increasing revenue opportunities. Furthermore, the integrated newsletter feature enables establishments to reach out to a broader audience and provide updates on new menu items, seasonal promotions, or special events. A coupon generator can also be integrated, allowing restaurants to distribute exclusive discounts to customers, encouraging repeat visits and brand loyalty.

To facilitate efficient communication between customers and the food industry, the smart city system can incorporate a contact form feature. This feature enables individuals to directly communicate with restaurants for inquiries, feedback, or special requests, fostering a personalized and responsive customer experience.

Moreover, the smart city system can incorporate an affiliate system as described in this book, allowing restaurants to collaborate with other businesses within the city ecosystem. Through strategic partnerships, restaurants can cross-promote offerings with hotels, tour operators, or entertainment venues, enabling them to attract new customers and increase their visibility.

By providing reservation and ordering capabilities to the food industry within the smart city, either through integration with existing systems or as an adjunct to the traveller-centric platform, the city can create a vibrant and interconnected dining ecosystem. This not only enhances the convenience and satisfaction of residents and visitors but also supports the growth and prosperity of the local food industry.

Rental Reservations

A smart city system designed for tourists presents numerous opportunities to enhance their experience. One essential feature is the ability to conveniently rent various modes of transportation and equipment, such as bicycles, watercraft, cars, and other specialized equipment. This inclusion allows tourists to explore the city and its surroundings with ease and flexibility.

To effectively manage this rental system, it should possess a robust inventory management capability, capable of handling a wide range of inventory types and availability relationships. The system must be configured to manage physical inventory, enabling rentals on an hourly, half-day, full-day, overnight, or for multiple days or hours, catering to diverse visitor preferences.

Furthermore, integration with resellers, sales agents, and affiliate programs is crucial. The city reservation system should seamlessly connect with these entities, facilitating collaboration and streamlining the inventory, commission, pricing, and packaging aspects. This integration ensures a cohesive ecosystem where stakeholders can effectively work together to provide the best possible offerings for tourists.

Moreover, the smart city system should be designed to allow other suppliers to easily integrate and sell their products and services. Whether it's boats, kayaks, jet ski rentals, or slip rentals, any item or experience that visitors may wish to rent should be seamlessly accessible through this traveller-centric system. This open integration approach encourages a diverse marketplace, providing tourists with a wide range of options and fostering healthy competition among suppliers.

Overall, a smart city system designed as a must-have tourist item has the potential to transform the way visitors experience and explore a city. By offering a comprehensive rental system for various modes of transportation and equipment, integrated with reservation systems and collaborating with stakeholders, the system becomes a central hub for tourists to access a wide array of offerings conveniently. This traveller-centric approach encourages exploration, enhances convenience, and contributes to an enriched tourism experience within the smart city.

E-commerce POS

Expanding on the idea of incorporating rentals into the system, I would recommend an e-commerce solution for physical products as an adjunct service on the city website, and there are several key aspects to consider.

Firstly, this platform can serve as a hub for selling unique tourist or popular items within the city. By showcasing and offering these products online, the city can tap into the potential of attracting a broader customer base, including both residents and visitors. This not only promotes local businesses but also enhances the overall tourism experience by providing convenient access to city-specific merchandise.

Furthermore, the e-commerce platform can also facilitate the sale of gift certificates online. This feature allows customers to purchase and send gift certificates digitally, providing a hassle-free gifting experience. By offering this service, the city enables individuals to support local businesses and promote their products while offering recipients the flexibility to choose their preferred items.

To ensure the success of this e-commerce initiative, it is crucial to incorporate a flexible technology infrastructure that can adapt to changing market needs. By investing in a robust and scalable platform, the city can respond rapidly to market trends, incorporate new features, and provide an optimized user experience for both customers and businesses.

A customer-centric approach to fulfilment and channel management is vital to creating a positive shopping experience. This involves streamlining order processing, optimizing inventory management, and ensuring efficient product delivery. Additionally, implementing enhanced individual customer pricing can personalize the shopping experience by tailoring prices based on customer preferences, loyalty, or other relevant factors.

Effective channel management strategies are essential for maximizing the reach and impact of the e-commerce platform. By leveraging technology, the city can establish partnerships with local businesses, tour operators, and other stakeholders to expand distribution channels and increase product visibility. These strategies may include affiliate programs, strategic alliances, or even integration with existing online marketplaces.

To establish individual or micro-level pricing for groups of customers, the e-commerce platform should incorporate dynamic pricing capabilities. This technology enables the city to adjust prices based on factors such as demand, market conditions, or customer segments. By implementing intelligent pricing algorithms, the platform can optimize revenue while remaining competitive and appealing to a wide range of customers.

Automated customer communication is essential for providing real-time updates on order status and enhancing overall customer service. By sending automated notifications and allowing secure customer login, individuals can easily track their account information and stay informed about their order status. This not only reduces the need for customer inquiries but also increases overall customer satisfaction and loyalty.

To boost sales and customer engagement, the e-commerce platform should support configurable products, cross-selling, and up-selling opportunities. By allowing customers to customize certain products, suggest complementary items, or provide special promotions, the platform can enhance the shopping experience and encourage higher-value purchases. Additionally, incorporating the ability to redeem coupons and participate in loyalty programs can further incentivize customers and drive repeat business.

As such, integrating an e-commerce platform for physical products on the city website offers numerous advantages. By showcasing unique city-specific items, selling gift certificates online, and utilizing flexible technology infrastructure, the city can enhance economic growth, support local businesses, and provide a convenient shopping experience for both residents and tourists. Incorporating customer-centric features, dynamic pricing strategies, automated communication, and advanced marketing techniques further ensures the success of this initiative, ultimately benefiting both the city and its customers.

Ridesharing Apps

Ridesharing has become an integral part of today's economy, revolutionizing the way people commute and travel. In this rapidly evolving landscape, developers who harness the power of ridesharing APIs are playing a crucial role in helping businesses stay competitive and meet the evolving needs of their customers. Integrating existing ridesharing applications into a smart city's traveller-centric system can offer significant advantages, not only in terms of cost-effectiveness but also in enhancing the overall user experience.

By incorporating ridesharing APIs into their applications, businesses can provide their customers with seamless access to popular ridesharing services like Uber and Lyft. This integration empowers customers by enabling them to conveniently obtain cost estimates and make informed decisions about their travel arrangements from within a single application. Gone are the days of juggling multiple apps or websites to compare prices or hail a ride. With ridesharing APIs, customers can streamline their transportation needs, saving time and effort.

Moreover, integrating ridesharing APIs with other transit and parking elements of a smart city system can significantly alleviate traffic congestion and improve the flow of travel within the city. By incorporating ridesharing options into a comprehensive mobility framework, travellers can seamlessly transition between different modes of transportation, such as buses, trains, and rideshares. This integration promotes efficient and sustainable travel choices, benefiting both commuters and the environment.

The advantages of ridesharing APIs extend beyond the realm of business and commuter convenience. Healthcare organizations can leverage these APIs, such as the Google rideshare APIs, to enhance the patient experience and improve appointment punctuality. By allowing users to select preferred routes and providing an estimated time of arrival, ridesharing APIs enable patients to plan their journeys more effectively, ensuring they arrive on time for their medical appointments. This improved punctuality can lead to increased efficiency in healthcare facilities, reducing waiting times and enhancing overall patient satisfaction.

Additionally, patients can avoid the hassle of searching for parking spaces near healthcare facilities by utilizing ridesharing services. By reserving rides in advance and relying on ridesharing APIs, patients can eliminate the stress of finding parking, especially in crowded urban areas. This not only saves time but also contributes to a smoother and more seamless healthcare experience.

It follows that ridesharing APIs have emerged as indispensable tools for developers and businesses looking to remain competitive in today's fast-paced economy. The integration of these APIs into a smart city's transportation ecosystem can enhance the overall user experience, alleviate congestion, and promote efficient travel flows within the city As technology continues to advance, leveraging the power of ridesharing APIs will become increasingly vital for organizations and cities striving to meet the evolving needs of their customers and residents.

Unleashing the Travel Industry's Potential: Online Travel Platforms

Online travel agencies (OTAs) are travel companies that sell various tourism products directly to travellers on booking websites with online travel agency software.

While the share of online booking is constantly growing, OTAs become more concerned about performance and seek the best travel software for their reservation systems.

In addition to specific technical requirements to meet, travel website software should have a user-friendly interface and many features to attract demanding tourists and experienced web surfers. For example, many tourists are interested in booking all tourism products on one website, including flights, hotels, transfers, railway tickets, excursions, and more.

The OTAs enterprise management system must be able to do many complicated tasks simultaneously: manage allotments and prices, set commissions and markups, create invoices, support extended loyalty programs, provide ticket capabilities and others. An important requirement is a possibility of efficiently managing reseller and commissionable programs that may be highly beneficial for the OTA's business.

Online travel agencies need to promote their services effectively, and technology is crucial for overall performance. A modern travel booking solution cannot succeed without an improved dynamic cache and advanced load balancing to enable fast search and price comparison.

Travel Agent Reservation System

One of the key differentiating features between basic reservation software and professional reservation software systems available in the market today is the ability to provide integrated Reservation Software for Travel Agents. This advanced functionality allows third-party resellers, such as travel agents, to seamlessly view and control their bookings, leading to enhanced efficiency and streamlined operations.

Within each module of the reservation software system, a dedicated Travel Agent Reservation System component is incorporated to ensure real-time updates of rate contracting and allotments. This component greatly improves the efficiency of managing contracts and ensures that travel agents always have access to up-to-date information on rates and availability.

To ensure secure access and personalized experiences, each travel agent or reseller is assigned a unique username and password. These credentials define their accounts, including information on the products they can offer, commissions they are entitled to, and credit limits assigned to them. By logging in with their username and password, travel agents can access and manage their accounts seamlessly.

For larger travel agents or travel agent companies, the reservation software system offers the flexibility to establish credit limits and payment schemes. This allows these companies to not only manage their operations efficiently but also assign unique username and password credentials to their internal or third-party travel agents. By doing so, these agents can utilize the total credit limit allocated to the travel agent company, further streamlining the booking and payment processes.

In addition to credit limits and account management, the reservation software system also facilitates direct access to contracted rates and discounts for each travel agent. By assigning a username and password to each agent, the system enables them to log in and access a wide selection of hotels, tours, transit options, and rental products. These products are offered at commissionable rates, and the entire booking process can be completed in a single checkout, providing a seamless experience for travel agents and their customers.

To cater to the diverse needs of travel agents and third-party resellers, a truly traveller-centric reservation software system should offer a fully integrated system. This means providing a comprehensive set-up that allows the customization of commission structures and various payment-related access points for travel agents and resellers. By offering this level of flexibility, the system empowers agents to tailor their payment processes according to their business models, ensuring a mutually beneficial relationship with the software provider.

As such, the integration of Travel Agent Reservation Software within a reservation software system sets apart the professional offerings in the market. By providing features such as real-time updates, personalized access, credit limits, commissionable rates, and flexible payment options, the system ensures efficient operations, seamless experiences, and mutually beneficial relationships between travel agents, resellers, and the software provider.

Affiliate Programs

One way to further expand marketing opportunities online is by implementing a comprehensive affiliate program based on a Pay per Sale model for both products and reservation items. This program will allow the company to collaborate with affiliates who can promote the brand and drive sales, thereby increasing online visibility and reaching a wider audience.

To maximize the effectiveness of the affiliate program, it is important to customize and tailor hybrid partnerships that promote brand loyalty with super affiliates and travel websites. These partnerships can be formed by offering special incentives and exclusive benefits to top-performing affiliates, encouraging them to continue promoting the company's products and services.

To efficiently manage the affiliate program, it is essential to have a well-designed system in place. This system should include a variety of anti-fraud protections to safeguard against fraudulent activities and ensure fair commission payouts. Additionally, a complete administration interface and a partner management section should be implemented. This interface will enable the company to communicate with affiliates via email, as well as enable, disable, or delete affiliate accounts as necessary.

A key component of the affiliate program is the availability of detailed statistics and reporting. The system should provide comprehensive data on referred orders and commissions earned, allowing the company to monitor the performance of affiliates and identify areas for improvement. Furthermore, the program should support unlimited banners and text banners, giving affiliates the flexibility to choose the promotional materials that best suit their websites and target audience.

To make it easier for affiliates to participate in the program, the software should automatically generate HTML banners and text link codes. These codes can be easily embedded by affiliates into their websites, allowing them to track referrals and earn commissions seamlessly.

Additionally, the affiliate program should feature an intuitive affiliate interface where potential affiliates can sign up for the program. Upon signing up, visitors should receive a unique URL that they can use to advertise the traveller-centric website. This personalized URL will enable the company to accurately track the source of referrals and attribute commissions accordingly.

To keep affiliates engaged and informed about their performance, a dedicated page should be provided that displays detailed statistics for affiliates. This page will showcase information such as the number of referred orders and the commissions earned, allowing affiliates to track their progress and earnings effectively.

By implementing these design suggestions, the company can establish a robust and effective affiliate program that not only expands marketing opportunities online but also fosters brand loyalty, provides comprehensive management tools, and offers valuable insights through detailed statistics and reporting.

Online Contracting Rate Distribution

The benefits of utilizing "online contracting" and "rate distribution" for managing a large number of travel agents and corporate clients are numerous. These features empower hotels, tour operators, rental companies, transit providers, and others to easily establish rates and allocations within the system. Once approved, any authorized travel agent can immediately access the system, view availability, and make reservations.

There are three methods by which resellers and travel agents can interact with the system:

1. Discounted Rate Purchases: Resellers have the option to purchase your products at a discounted rate, determined by a percentage of your choosing. They can then utilize or resell these products under their name.

2. Logo/Link Integration: When resellers receive a confirmation email, it includes your selected logo or link graphic along with a unique ID string. By placing this logo on their website, visitors can click on it and directly access your website to complete reservations. While the reservation is made under the customer's name, the transaction is attributed to the travel agent through their embedded Travel Agent ID number.

3. Secure Sales Link: Travel agents can access a dedicated sales link on your website to book reservations for their customers. After their secure login details are authenticated, they can choose from their list of customers or create a new client profile if necessary. To ensure proper credit for the transaction, travel agents must go through the special sales link, which embeds their ID number in the transaction.

Once again, the reservation is made under the customer's name but credited to the travel agent.

The system should provide the admin with access to travel agent reports for commission purposes. Each reseller or agent can access their report using their unique username and password.

Login credentials issued by the company can be distributed to multiple reservation staff members as determined by the travel agent. This allows each staff member to view real-time rates and availability without waiting for rate adjustments from a supervisor.

Additionally, the system should allow for the establishment of credit limits for agents. The system will automatically check purchases against available credit, ensuring that agents do not exceed their limits. Payment information can be recorded, and comprehensive reports are accessible in the agent's online account as well as for the admin.

With online reservations, there is no need to wait for a confirmation. Reservation staff members can instantly confirm reservations rather than submitting reservation requests or forms.

Online contracting ensures equal treatment for all clients. Once approved, travel agents and corporate clients receive a unique login and password combination that grants them 24/7 access to rates and allocations. They can make reservations and receive instant confirmations at their agreed-upon rates.

Accounting & Reporting Data Requirement

Managing the sales activities of travel agents entails addressing a multitude of essential reports. These reports encompass a range of crucial aspects such as account reconciliation, commission calculations, travel agent accounts, customer invoicing, and more. However, it is worth noting that additional reports can be generated based on specific requests or as necessitated by the diverse range of methods available for exporting report data from most databases that support traveller-centric operations.

One of the fundamental reports in the realm of travel agent sales is account reconciliation. This report plays a vital role in ensuring that financial transactions between the travel agency and agents are accurately recorded and balanced. It provides a comprehensive overview of the monetary exchanges, ensuring that any discrepancies or errors can be identified and rectified promptly.

Another significant report pertains to commission calculations. As travel agents often earn commissions on the sales they generate, it is crucial to have a systematic approach to calculating these commissions accurately. This report enables the travel agency to determine the appropriate commissions owed to each agent based on their sales performance. By providing transparent and reliable commission information, this report fosters trust and maintains healthy relationships with travel agents.

In addition to monitoring account reconciliation and commissions, travel agent accounts are another key area that requires careful consideration. The travel agency needs to maintain detailed records of individual travel agent accounts, including important information such as contact details, payment preferences, and transaction histories. By regularly reviewing these accounts, the agency can ensure that all pertinent information is up-to-date and accessible for efficient communication and financial processing.

Customer invoicing is yet another critical aspect of travel agent sales management. It involves generating accurate and timely invoices for customers based on their bookings and travel arrangements. These invoices should clearly outline the services rendered, associated costs, payment terms, and any applicable taxes or fees. The customer invoicing report assists in streamlining the billing process, reducing errors, and ensuring that customers receive accurate and professional invoices.

While the aforementioned reports cover several essential aspects of travel agent sales, it is essential to recognize that other reports can be developed based on specific needs or as the industry evolves. Most modern databases supporting traveller-centric operations offer various methods for exporting data, enabling the creation of custom reports. These reports can encompass diverse metrics such as sales performance, customer preferences, market trends, or any other data points deemed valuable for strategic decision-making and enhancing overall operational efficiency.

I must stress that managing travel agent sales entails a comprehensive consideration of multiple reports. Account reconciliation, commission calculations, travel agent accounts, and customer invoicing are among the essential reports required for efficient sales operations. Moreover, the flexibility of exporting data from modern databases allows for the creation of additional reports tailored to specific needs, providing valuable insights for optimizing performance and adapting to the ever-evolving travel industry landscape.

Transforming Urban Parking: Intelligent Solutions for Smart Cities

This chapter outlines the generic concept of using a Traveller-centric system to set up an intelligent car parking service in a smart city environment.

The world is constantly looking to technology to run its services more efficiently; Towns and cities are starting to utilize modern technology to become smart destinations, whether it's in offering live updates of their transport network, or in real-time tourist information to anyone that visits. One of the most essential aspects of a city or town is its transportation, and that includes traffic congestion and parking.

As the world's population soars, so does the number of cars on the roads, and this is particularly problematic when it comes to busy urban areas. Insufficient parking and traffic congestion are just two of the consequences of this change, and this is why cities are starting to look to Smart Parking for a solution.

Smart parking aims to utilize the world of technology, bringing it to the world of parking. In busy areas where parking can be difficult, smart parking offers real-time information regarding vacant spaces, allowing drivers to determine where they can park without having to drive around looking for a space.

This can be considered an important application of the 'Internet of Things (IoT) paradigm. This is a type of service that will become an integral part of a generic IoT operational platform within a Smart city due to its pure business-orientated features.

Using the capabilities of Traveller-centric systems integrated with the application of sensor technology would provide an enterprise-based or company-based platform to improve competitiveness and service assurance of market-oriented IT enterprises and companies operating within the parking industry.

A system used as the middleware behind an intelligent car parking system would constitute an important part of a smart city, with the primary purpose to find, allocate, reserve, and provide the best available car parking lot to each user who is driving a car in a particular area.

Valuable add-on functionality could be the provision of navigation instructions to the driver for reaching the lot.

Existing car parking systems are not very efficient as they do not provide the best service for finding the nearest available car parking lot. At the sensor layer, most car parking lots do not provide this sort of functionality.

With a smart Traveller-centric reservation system it's proposed that sensors would be used to detect the car parking lot occupancy allied at the communication layer, acting as a multi-agent system facilitating a car parking locator service whereby users are provided with a personalized service based on their location and mobile devices capabilities.

The city and parking lot owners would be able to integrate their lot locations, space availability, etc. into the systems middleware.

Car owners would be able to search online for available parking locations, availability and parking location, if necessary pay and reserve that location online and then be provided directions using integrated Google maps, etc. to drive to that location.

The system would allow cities and parking lot operators to rapidly develop intelligent car parking systems which can serve the users in an Always Best Connected and Best Served manner.

With the appropriate integrations in place, a smart city can establish a multimodal door-to-door trip planning, reservation and ticketing system for their city of choice, which could also include accommodation, activities, rental operations and parking, etc.

Cyber-Physical Systems (CPS)

Cyber-Physical Systems (CPS) are systems that have been engineered to interact between physical and computational components. Typically, this computation and communication are deeply embedded in and interact with physical processes to add new capabilities and characteristics to physical systems.

Typically a CPS has been built using closed architecture in a domain-specific format with self-contained resources. This approach is inadequate for smart city solutions, which are typically multi-domain and cut across conventional organizational and infrastructure boundaries to develop solutions.

At the heart of the CPS is the fact that it is a system with links to the physical world, (e.g., Via sensors, actuators or other digitally controlled analogue devices.) to the world of information processing.

These diverse constituent parts are required to collaborate to create some form of global behaviour. Such a software system integrates communications technology and the sensors or actuators that interact with the real world, often including embedded technologies.

One such example can be a fully integrated parking reservation, ticketing and payment solution using electronic gates, and embedded sensors within the actual parking spaces both in parking lots and at the roadside. This information is communicated to the software reservation system and propagated through the Internet via mobile, etc. devices for users to select available parking spots.

Reservation Based Smart Parking

One of the most exciting developments in smart parking is the ability to reserve a vacant space before getting to the actual area. By reserving a free parking spot, drivers can head to their destination knowing they will be able to park, therefore alleviating some of the congestion on the roads.

Smart technology can even determine the price of parking using a dynamic pricing scheme. This takes into account the demand for parking space and the availability in the surrounding area, giving an updated price to each driver as they are using the platform.

It has been estimated in some cities that cars searching for parking spaces can account for a 40% rise in traffic, so there has never been a better time to look to smart technology in the hope it will have a positive impact on traffic congestion and the environment.

Calendar-Driven Multiple Placement Selection Engine with Active Seat Maps and Layout GUI

Dynamic seat mapping allows for the optimized allocation and utilization of seats in various public spaces such as parks, theatres, stadiums, parking and public transportation. By dynamically assigning seats based on real-time availability, the system ensures that seats are used efficiently and effectively, reducing wasted space.

With dynamic seat mapping, users can instantly view the availability of seats in different venues or modes of transportation. This information can be accessed through mobile apps or online platforms, enabling users to make informed decisions about their reservations or bookings. Real-time availability data helps avoid overbooking and ensures a seamless user experience.

The reservation and booking system for seats, parking, and physical layouts requires thinking about the following features:

1 - Calendar-Driven Multiple Placement Selection Engine:

- Utilizes a calendar-based system for selecting multiple placements, such as seats, hotel rooms, or other placements.
- Provides an intuitive graphical user interface (GUI) for easy selection using a mouse or keyboard.
- Supports Voyager hotel, tour, rental, and ticketing software.

2 - Active Seat Maps with Layout GUI:

- Offers a powerful colour-coded graphical display of seating or placement options.
- Allows customers to provide their graphical layouts for a personalized experience.

- Enables easy and precise selection of seats, hotel rooms, or other placements through intuitive mouse movements and clicks.
- Facilitates online reservations and ticket sales.

3 - Tier-Released Seating:

- Accommodates different customer types (residents, tourists, and commercial vehicles) on ferry and bus routes.
- Implements tiered releases of seating and space availability.
- Ensures equal access to reserve space for customers planning or closer to the sailing date.

4 - Easy Administration and Client Booking:

- Admin-friendly setup and control features.
- User-friendly interface for clients to easily book and make reservations.

5 - Active Maps for Property or Equipment Reservations:

- Interactive maps of the property or equipment that can be clicked on to make reservations.
- Displays unit availability through status colours (e.g., red or green).
- Supports various booking functions, including individual and group bookings, and availability search by specific dates.

6 - Integration of Customer-Specific Graphics:

- Integrates customer-provided graphics into the software's selection engine.
- Creates an easy-to-read graphical view of hotels, venues,

seating layouts, etc.

- Provides a quick view of available inventory by date, placement, price tier, and inventory type.

7 - Advanced Information Presentation:

- Presents information graphically, enabling selection and sale of single seats, marina docking spaces, campground locations, hotel rooms, etc.
- Enables fast and efficient client service by providing a wealth of information.

8 - Dynamic Seat or Place Mapping:

- Supports dynamic planning, optimization, and adjustment of the seat or place allocations.
- Automatically distributes and reschedules seat quotas based on real-time events.
- Interfaces with the administrative system to notify customers about schedule changes, and cancellations, and perform required accounting and pricing functions.

9 - Multi-Layered Dynamic Seat Mapping:

- Allows central office seat quota fixation and adjustment.
- Enables modification of seat quotas at the station level and synchronization with the central system based on local resources and conditions.

Integration of Existing Parking Apps Such As WaytoPark

Although most current apps do not support parking sensor technology, a basic automated parking system can be readily established that does not use the reservation of spaces. Integrating an existing app, such as the WayToPark car parking app into a traveller-centric smart city reservation and ticketing system, while combining its use with artificial intelligence (AI), can significantly enhance the parking experience for users. Here's a step-by-step guide on the best method to achieve this integration:

1. Define objectives and requirements: Clearly outline the goals of integrating the WayToPark app with the smart city reservation and ticketing system. Identify the desired features, such as real-time parking availability, personalized recommendations, automated payment processing, and AI-driven predictive analytics.

2. Establish data sharing protocols: Ensure that the WayToPark app and the smart city reservation and ticketing system can communicate and share relevant data seamlessly. Define the necessary APIs (Application Programming Interfaces) or data exchange formats to facilitate data transfer between the systems.

3. Implement real-time parking availability: Enable real-time updates of parking available through the integration. The WayToPark app should receive live information from the smart city reservation and ticketing system, allowing users to view parking spots in real time, including availability, rates, and other relevant details.

4. Enable personalized recommendations: Utilize AI algorithms to provide personalized parking recommendations to users based on their preferences, historical data, and real-time conditions. Incorporate machine learning techniques to analyze user behaviour, parking patterns, and contextual data to suggest the most suitable parking options.

5. Automate payment processing: Integrate the payment systems of both the WayToPark app and the smart city

reservation and ticketing system. Users should be able to pay for parking seamlessly within the app, using various payment methods such as credit cards, mobile wallets, or pre-loaded accounts. AI algorithms can be used to optimize the payment process, including fraud detection and secure transaction handling.

6. Implement AI-driven predictive analytics: Utilize AI techniques to analyze historical parking data, user patterns, and external factors (e.g., events, and weather) to provide predictive analytics. This can help users plan their parking, estimate parking availability during specific times, and suggest alternative parking options in case of high demand.

7. Ensure seamless user experience: Focus on creating a seamless user experience throughout the integration. Design an intuitive interface that combines the functionalities of the WayToPark app and the smart city reservation and ticketing system, providing a unified platform for users to search, reserve, pay for parking, and access additional services.

8. Test and refine the integration: Conduct rigorous testing to ensure the integration works smoothly across various devices and platforms. Gather user feedback and iterate on the integration to address any usability issues, bugs, or performance concerns.

9. Implement security and privacy measures: Prioritize security and privacy by implementing robust measures to protect user data and ensure secure transactions. Comply with relevant data protection regulations and industry best practices to build user trust in the integrated system.

10. Continuous improvement and innovation: Monitor user feedback, gather data, and leverage AI capabilities to continuously improve the integrated system. Explore innovative features and technologies to enhance the parking

experience and stay ahead of evolving user needs.

By following this method, integrating the WayToPark car parking app into a traveller-centric smart city reservation and ticketing system while incorporating AI can create a comprehensive and user-friendly solution for efficient and intelligent parking management in smart cities.

Securing the Journey: The Evolution of Passenger Safety and Online Reservation Systems

One of the major failings of most online reservation systems with passenger security and online reservation systems is the inability to adequately handle passenger security.

Passenger security in the airline industry is probably the top end of the security chain due to the large number of flights, passengers and risk potential.

Smaller tour operators, bus and ferry operators, tend to issue tickets online or at boarding terminals without any real security checks.

Bus routes internal to a country, tend to be less security conscious as there have been few specific major acts of terrorism carried out on such transportation types.

Of increasing, importance is ferry services that operate in coastal waters and utilize large shipping waterways and ports for that passenger services.

The law in most countries considers ferries considered fixed guideways. There are three different route designations commonly used within the ferry system.

1 – Fixed routes, which are also called closed-loop routes have a fixed point designating the beginning and end. Each trip may take a slightly different course, but the beginning and end of the route are located at fixed points

2 – Segmented routes, which are, also called open loop routes which are portions of the fixed route with multiple stops.

3 – Metropolitan routes serve metropolitan areas and carry the majority of the national ferry system passengers in most countries.

It should be noted, that in addition to the above route designations, ferry services might be categorized as regular or express services. Another note is that the Traveller-centric Enterprise system handles all of the above route requirements.

As the majority of most ferry routes are considered essential service routes, meaning that possibly there are no other modes of transportation available to the specific destination serviced, then such services are often considered the lifelines of island communities and could be the potential risk to acts of terrorism.

With this in mind, it is essential to provide additional security to the passenger or customer profile in a Traveller-centric system. So what are reasonable security requirements that could be integrated within a reservation system that would also be useful and can be connected to external security equipment by the appropriate Tour, Ferry, Aircraft or Bus Company?

My research indicated that the transportation industry authentication systems are usually characterized by three factors:

1 – One something that a passenger knows, such as a username/a password;

2 – Something that a passenger would have, such as an ID badge, passport, driving license, etc.;

3 – and/or something that a passenger is, such as their fingerprints or their face.

Many agencies are starting to implement the third factor, biometric applications, in their authentication processes.

The user client profile within your reservation and the ticketing system should be designed so it can contain three photo ID files. These could consist of a photo, fingerprint scan and retinal scan.

Passenger information can also include passport numbers, height weight, no-fly list details and other typical MARSEC passenger data.

This information when required can be selectively printed onto pre-boarding and boarding passes or viewed on screens or mobile devices designed by clients for their security services.

These features should be incorporated in a 'Safe Travel' module that is part of your passenger profile system.

Eliminating Usernames and Passwords Using Blockchain

Currently, with most e-commerce systems, online authentication relies on a password or rare occasions the use of Two-factor authentication.

When you have to enter only your username or password, that's considered a single-factor authentication. Two-factor authentication requires the user to have three types of credentials before being able to access an account.

This may be something in the form of a personal identification number PIN, something you have, such as an ATM card, phone, etc.

Or something you are, such as a biometric like a fingerprint, iris scan or facial recognition.

Two-factor authentication, adds an extra step to a basic login procedure. The second factor makes your account more secure, in theory.

Enterprises with software that implements two-factor authentication can provide users with a better user experience and achieve stronger security.

The problem with these methods is that passwords are notoriously insecure and Two-factor authentication generally relies on sending a code over SMS or a third-party service. Using biometrics requires that a fingerprint scan, iris scan or facial recognition scan be validated.

A solution to this problem could be the blockchain.

No need to maintain a central database full of usernames and passwords that are vulnerable to breaches by hackers.

The blockchain is the secure distributed ledger technology first created to track claim ownership.

The blockchain offers a promise of a trusted record that can reduce fraud. An advantage to using blockchain as a means of controlling identity information is the ability to extend security to your enterprise's entire ecosystem.

For many companies, logging into online ticketing, e-commerce or POS type system requires identity authentication to go beyond existing employees.

It has to be extended to partners, sales channels, sales agents and customers who log into the company's system and are then able to use blockchain to verify their identities.

A blockchain ID is a unique identifier that is secured by a blockchain a user can cryptographically link their blockchain ID to a profile containing arbitrary information, e.g., name customer details, sales information and history, discounts and reward points, etc.

Identity Management

There is a definite requirement for better identity management on the web. The ability to verify an individual's identity when logging into an e-commerce system is a linchpin of the customer's access and of past and future transactions that happen online within that system.

With the integration of distributed ledger technology within a large multivendor, multisite multi-module system, keeping accurate records in such a distributed system, will be a common part of the identity management ecosystem and help improve all aspects of it.

By combining the decentralized blockchain principle with identity verification, a digital ID can be created to act as a digital watermark, which can then be assigned, to every online transaction within the main system and all associated websites and subsystems.

Passenger Profiles

Traveller-centric Passenger Profiles provides a powerful tool for customers to interact with your company by creating profiles. They can store all of their contact details online so that when they return to make bookings the system recognizes them and automatically fills in the booking forms. They can also store passport details for advance passenger information, request to be kept informed by SMS or Email and sign up for newsletters.

Call centre staff can search for passenger profiles based on past bookings as well as user names and contact details to view possible profiles of passengers. They can then use the information to complete bookings as well as see the preferences of the passengers.

Marketing teams can use the extensive reporting module to extract data from the system and use it in marketing campaigns based on intelligent filtering such as routes, seasons, customer location etc. Use the in-built SMS and Email modules for promotional campaigns or export to a 3rd party system.

Here are some considerations and requirements for designing such a database:

1. Information Capture: The database should be designed to capture various passenger details, such as:
2. Personal Information: Full name, gender, date of birth, contact information (phone number, email), nationality, passport details, frequent flyer program details (if applicable). Also, it is advisable to look at including physical characteristics as outlined in the passenger security and passenger biometrics sections of this book.
3. Travel Preferences: Seat preference (window, aisle), meal preference (vegetarian, kosher, etc.), special needs (medical requirements, wheelchair assistance), language preference.
4. Travel History: Previous flights, destinations, loyalty program status.
5. Data Security: The passenger profile database should prioritize data security and adhere to privacy regulations such as the General Data Protection Regulation (GDPR) or local laws. It should employ encryption, access controls, and other security measures to protect passenger information.

6. Centralized Storage: All passenger profiles should be stored in a centralized database, allowing easy access and retrieval of passenger information across different modules of the traveller-centric reservation system.

7. Scalability: The database design should be scalable to accommodate a growing number of passenger profiles. It should handle increasing data volumes without compromising system performance.

8. Data Integrity: The database should ensure data integrity by implementing measures such as data validation, normalization, and referential integrity. This helps maintain the consistency and accuracy of passenger information.

9. Integration: The passenger profile database should integrate with other modules of the traveller-centric reservation system, such as the booking engine, check-in system, loyalty program, and customer relationship management (CRM) system. This allows seamless sharing of passenger data across various touchpoints.

10. Analytics and Personalization: The database should support analytical capabilities to derive insights from passenger profiles. It can help identify trends, preferences, and behaviour patterns, enabling personalized offers and recommendations.

11. Performance: The database should be designed to handle concurrent access and queries efficiently to ensure a smooth user experience. Proper indexing, query optimization, and database tuning may be required to achieve optimal performance.

12. Compliance: The passenger profile database should comply with industry standards and regulations related to data protection, privacy, and storage.

13. Backup and Recovery: Regular backups and a robust disaster

recovery plan should be implemented to safeguard passenger data and ensure business continuity in case of system failures or data loss.

Quantifying the requirements for designing a passenger profile database depends on various factors such as the expected number of passengers, the frequency of data updates, and the specific features and functionalities of the traveler-centric reservation system. This may involve estimating the storage capacity needed based on the average size of a passenger profile, projected growth in the number of profiles, and the retention period for historical data. Additionally, performance requirements should be defined in terms of expected response times, concurrency levels, and transaction throughput.

It's essential to work closely with database administrators, system architects, and relevant stakeholders to accurately quantify the requirements and ensure the passenger profile database meets the specific needs of the traveller-centric reservation system.

Voice-Enabled Travel Search

As travel research increasingly moves to mobile devices, one must begin to look at the convergence and the value of integrating voice-activated and Artificial Intelligence technology into the travel search and booking world.

Here are some advantages and possibilities:

1. Seamless User Experience: Voice-activated technology allows users to interact with travel search and booking platforms using natural language. It eliminates the need for typing or navigating through complex interfaces, making the process more intuitive and user-friendly.

2. Personalized Recommendations: AI can analyze user preferences, past travel history, and other relevant data to provide personalized recommendations. By integrating voice-activated technology, users can have a conversation with the

AI assistant, specifying their preferences and receiving tailored suggestions for flights, accommodations, activities, and more.

3. Instant Voice-Activated Bookings: Voice-activated technology combined with AI can enable users to book travel services instantly. Users can simply speak their preferences and the AI assistant can make reservations, and book flights, hotels, rental cars, and other services on their behalf, eliminating the need for manual input and streamlining the booking process.

4. Real-Time Travel Information: AI-powered voice assistants can provide travellers with real-time information about flights, delays, gate changes, traffic conditions, weather updates, and other relevant details. Users can receive this information by simply asking questions, allowing them to stay informed and make timely decisions during their travels.

5. Multilingual Support: Voice-activated technology can provide multilingual support, allowing users to search and book travel services in their preferred language. AI-powered translation capabilities can facilitate communication between travellers and travel platforms, breaking language barriers and making the process more accessible to a global audience.

6. Natural Language Understanding: AI-powered voice assistants can understand complex queries and provide accurate responses, enhancing the search capabilities of travel platforms. Users can ask detailed questions about travel destinations, local attractions, visa requirements, and more, receiving comprehensive and relevant information.

7. Virtual Travel Concierge: Voice-activated AI assistants can act as virtual travel concierges, offering assistance throughout the entire travel journey. They can provide recommendations for restaurants, attractions, and local events, offer packing

suggestions, suggest alternative travel options in case of disruptions, and provide 24/7 customer support, ensuring a personalized and hassle-free experience.

8. Voice-Activated Smart Speakers: Travel search and booking platforms can integrate with popular smart speakers, enabling users to make travel-related inquiries and bookings directly through devices like Amazon Echo or Google Home. This expands the accessibility of travel services, making them available in homes, hotels, and other locations.

However, it's important to address potential challenges and concerns when integrating voice-activated and AI technologies. These include privacy and data security, the accuracy of voice recognition, language understanding, and maintaining a balance between automation and human assistance to ensure a positive user experience.

Overall, the integration of voice-activated technology and AI into the travel search and booking world has the potential to revolutionize the industry, providing users with more personalized, efficient, and intuitive experiences.

Guest Access Module

To provide a seamless and user-friendly experience, it is imperative to empower users with the ability to manage their reservations autonomously. Users should have the freedom to cancel or modify their bookings without being dependent on administrative assistance. This level of control not only enhances user satisfaction but also streamlines the overall reservation process.

To facilitate this, an integrated Guest Access pathway should be implemented within the system. This pathway would allow registered users to log in to their accounts and effortlessly cancel any bookings they have made. By offering this functionality, users gain the flexibility to adjust their plans according to their needs, such as rescheduling their reservations for new dates or making other modifications.

By providing a self-service cancellation and modification feature, the system eliminates the hassle and potential delays associated with contacting administrators for such requests. Users can easily navigate through their accounts, access their reservation details, and make the necessary adjustments conveniently and efficiently.

Moreover, this integrated pathway should not only enable cancellations but also allow users to make new reservations on alternative dates or choose from available options. By integrating these capabilities, users can seamlessly transition from cancelling their previous booking to reserving a new one, all within the same intuitive interface.

The Guest Access pathway should prioritize security measures to safeguard user's personal information and ensure that only authorized individuals can access and modify reservations. Robust authentication mechanisms, such as username and password combinations or multi-factor authentication, should be implemented to protect user accounts from unauthorized access.

Overall, implementing an integrated Guest Access pathway empowers users to take control of their reservations, promoting a user-centric approach that reduces reliance on administrative assistance and enhances the overall efficiency and satisfaction of the reservation process.

Passenger Biometrics

I suggest developing an integrated passenger safe travel profile system with the following features:

1. Biometric Recognition System: Implement a real-time biometric recognition system that supports various biometric modalities such as face recognition, iris recognition, and fingerprint scanning. This system should capture biometric data from passengers and compare it with their existing profiles in the system.

2. Equipment Compatibility: Ensure that the software design interfaces seamlessly with a wide range of physical equipment available on the market today. This includes integrating biometric devices (such as cameras, iris scanners, and fingerprint scanners) and supporting their functionalities for capturing and processing biometric data.

3. Modes of Operation: The system should offer two modes of operation: database comparison and ID file comparison. In the database comparison mode, the captured biometric data is compared against the profiles stored in the system's database. In the ID file comparison mode, the system compares the captured data with the biometric information stored in the passenger's ID file.

4. Ticketing System: Develop a comprehensive ticketing system that supports various ticketing equipment, including printers, cameras, optical barcodes, and digital readers. This system should enable an online seat occupancy display, allowing passengers to view and select available seats during the ticketing process.

5. Merchant Gateways Integration: Integrate fully with merchant gateways to enable secure and seamless payment processing. This integration will enable passengers to make online payments for their tickets through various payment methods.

6. Ticket Generation: Provide the capability to generate tickets online or use preprinted tickets. The system should dynamically populate the tickets with relevant information such as seat details, personalized passenger information, and barcode or QR codes for easy validation and scanning.

7. Mobile Ticketing Support: Enable mobile ticketing by integrating with mobile devices. Passengers should have the option to receive their tickets digitally on their mobile

devices, allowing for convenient ticket access and validation.

Security measures within the proposed system rely on biometric encryption templates to securely store customer data in their profiles. When a customer places an order, the order details are encoded as a 2D barcode or QR code, etc., and the database stores the hashed value of the key associated with the customer's template. This key and the ticket are exclusively used for that specific order.

During the verification process at a terminal, the user's ticket information is scanned into the Traveller-centric system. The system then reads the ticket information and proceeds with either capturing a live biometric sample or applying the stored biometric template associated with that user to retrieve the key. The key is transmitted to the database, where it is compared to the stored version. Based on the outcome of this comparison, appropriate actions are taken to ensure security and authentication.

By incorporating these features, the suggested system will provide a seamless and secure travel experience for passengers, leveraging biometric recognition, efficient ticketing, and easy payment processing.

TSA Secure Flight Program

To ensure the highest level of security in domestic and international commercial air travel, the software must offer robust support for the Transportation Security Administration (TSA) Secure Flight Program. This support should be provided as a configurable option, allowing users to enable or disable the feature according to their specific needs.

The primary objective of the TSA Secure Flight Program is to strengthen the security measures implemented within the aviation industry by implementing improved watch list matching procedures. By utilizing advanced technologies and information analysis, the program aims to prevent potential threats and enhance passenger safety.

Under the guidelines set forth by the TSA Secure Flight Program, the Secure Flight Rule mandates that air carriers request certain information from passengers during the booking process. This information, referred to as Secure Flight Passenger Data (SFPD), is crucial for conducting thorough watch list matching and ensuring that individuals with potential security concerns are identified.

To comply with the TSA regulations, the software should include a comprehensive set of fields that can be completed when gathering Secure Flight Passenger Data. These fields may include, but are not limited to, the following:

1. Full Name: The passenger's complete legal name as it appears on the government-issued identification document they will be using for travel.
2. Date of Birth: The passenger's birthdate, which aids in accurately identifying individuals on watch lists.
3. Gender: The passenger's gender information, which can be utilized to further refine matching procedures.
4. Redress Number: If applicable, a unique identifier is provided to individuals who have previously experienced watch list matching issues.
5. Known Traveler Number: If the passenger is enrolled in a trusted traveller program, such as TSA PreCheck, this number can be entered to expedite the screening process.

To ensure compliance with the TSA Secure Flight Program, the software should be configured to request Secure Flight Passenger Data from passengers for all types of bookings. This includes reservations made online, through travel agencies, or via online booking agents. By consistently collecting this essential information, the software enables the airline or travel organization to fulfil its obligations under the Secure Flight Rule and maintain the highest level of security in the aviation industry.

Furthermore, the software should provide flexibility in terms of customization. Administrators should have the ability to enable or disable the requirement for Secure Flight Passenger Data collection based on their specific business needs and compliance obligations. This reconfigurability allows organizations to adapt the system to changing regulations and ensures seamless integration of the TSA Secure Flight Program within their operational processes.

By incorporating robust support for the TSA Secure Flight Program, including the ability to request and manage Secure Flight Passenger Data, the software enables airlines and travel organizations to contribute to the overall enhancement of aviation security. With accurate watch list matching and comprehensive passenger information, the industry can take proactive measures to identify potential threats, maintain passenger safety, and promote a secure travel experience for all.

Geofencing and Traveller-centric Paperless Ticketing

A Traveller-centric system should look at implementing multiple disruptive marketing solutions that cater to various business needs including the use of geo-fence in as an optimal solution to enhance mobile's influence on the travel sector.

As location-based targeting takes off and consumers increasing tendencies to book last-minute vacations or business trips on mobile, we can expect the travel and tourism sector to become even more did you tally inclined as wearables also take off.

Geo-fencing can be looked upon as a virtual perimeter drawn around any location on a map, and then you can target customers that enter that location. Typically using Google Maps or other mapping products, you can identify the area that you wish to geo-fence, and then create a particular region around the locations you wish to target.

Through various marketing approaches, you can provide an app to potential clients or existing users allowing the capability for that app to monitor for that particular geo-fence.

Geo-fences can be used to target customers in physical locations allowing you to trigger the right message, campaign, ticket purchases, etc. as users breach your particular geo-fence.

Using a Traveller-centric system as the reservation and ticketing central system allows applications to use geo-fence in a wide variety of situations.

One such use would be paperless ticketing using a mobile application. This would allow passengers who breach a geo-fence en route or upon entering a bus, train or ferry terminal, etc. to buy a ticket on the move and allow them to board with the ticket secured on their mobile phone without any requirement for printing the ticket.

The application would provide the necessary on-screen alerts to guide the passenger during the booking process. With Traveller-centric and support for a wide variety of merchant gateways payment could easily be included via the application itself.

The paperless journey ticket would be stored in the local loading system database in encrypted form and be subject to whatever rules are stored in the Traveller-centric rules engine.

This is of course just one example of the use of a Traveller-centric, geo-fencing and mobile application.

DCS (Departure Control System)

A Departure Control System (DCS), provides an integrated passenger handling service for small to medium-sized ferry, bus, tour and other transit passenger-type operations.

As part of a Traveller-centric reservation and ticketing system, it simplifies the entire check-in process from start to finish by requiring only a computer and an Internet connection. It's a feature that when fully implemented provides productivity features and real-time processing and keeps passenger service running as smoothly as possible.

DCS can assist its users in delivering rapid, cost-effective automated check-in and boarding as part of the Traveller-centric system.

Ideal for low-cost carriers, charter operations and point-to-point operators including ground tour and shuttle operators.

It should support real-time passenger validation for improved on-time performance with its support of a full range of devices for reading boarding passes including handheld scanners, boarding gate readers and self-boarding gates.

DCS as part of the system must be designed to use commodity hardware for printers and barcode scanners, readers, which cost much less than specialized hardware.

Sales agents can also scan barcodes on the boarding passes which update the DCS system as passengers arrive at the gate to be processed for their equipment boarding. Passengers may only board if the DCS matches the passenger to the appropriate tour or trip.

This eases and speeds up the customer check-in process, not only for transit operations but also can be used to improve entry flow to events, etc.

Unlocking the Future of Online Ticketing: Embracing Tomorrow's Possibilities

Online ticketing is bigger than ever, and with the market still expanding, we are looking at what the future holds for ticketing in the digital age.

A recent study found that mobile and online ticketing would soon account for a vast majority of ticket purchases across the world, with the market doubling by the year 20xx. This reach is also expected to expand across the globe, even into regions that are steadily increasing their technological capabilities, from Latin America and Africa to the Middle East.

One of the biggest trends in ticketing is mobile ticketing. It has been predicted that barcode and SMS-based ticketing solutions will become increasingly popular over the next few years. They have already proved popular within the transport industries, and they are set to take off within industries across the retail sector too. And with payment systems such as Apple Pay and Google Wallet becoming more widespread, it is expected that 1 in 3 ticketing purchases will be made via these means by 2024.

The future of ticketing in smart travel and smart cities is likely to be driven by advancements in technology and a shift towards more integrated and seamless experiences for travellers. Here are some key trends and possibilities for the future of ticketing:

1. Mobile Ticketing: Mobile ticketing has already gained popularity, and it is expected to become even more prevalent in the future. Travellers will be able to purchase and store tickets on their smartphones, eliminating the need for physical tickets or cards. This will provide convenience and

flexibility, allowing travellers to access their tickets anytime, anywhere.

2. Contactless Payments: With the rise of contactless payment systems like NFC (Near Field Communication) and RFID (Radio-Frequency Identification), ticketing will become more streamlined. Travellers will be able to use their smartphones or smart cards to tap and pay for tickets without the need for cash or physical cards. This technology can be integrated into various modes of transportation, including buses, trains, and subways.

3. Integrated Ticketing Systems: Smart cities will likely adopt integrated ticketing systems that allow travellers to use a single ticket or payment method across multiple modes of transportation. This means that a single ticket or pass can be used for buses, trains, trams, ferries, and other transportation services within a city or region. This integrated approach will simplify the ticketing process and encourage the use of public transportation.

4. Real-Time Ticketing and Dynamic Pricing: Ticketing systems will become more dynamic, leveraging real-time data to offer personalized and flexible ticketing options. For instance, pricing may vary based on demand and time of day, allowing travellers to choose the most cost-effective options. Real-time updates will also enable travellers to check schedules, delays, and availability on their devices, ensuring a smoother travel experience.

5. Seamless Intermodal Travel: The future of ticketing will focus on creating a seamless experience for travellers when switching between different modes of transportation. For example, a traveller can seamlessly transition from a bus to a train without needing to purchase separate tickets or go through multiple validation processes. This will encourage

the use of public transportation and make intermodal travel more efficient.

6. Data Integration and Analytics: Ticketing systems will leverage data analytics to gain insights into travel patterns, passenger flows, and demand. This information can be used to optimize routes, schedules, and pricing strategies, resulting in improved efficiency and reduced congestion. Data integration will also enable the sharing of information between transportation providers and authorities, allowing for better coordination and planning.

Overall, the future of ticketing in smart travel and smart cities will revolve around convenience, integration, and personalization. Technology will play a crucial role in creating a seamless and efficient travel experience, making it easier for individuals to navigate and access transportation services within cities and across different modes of travel.

Ticketing with RFIDS

RFID tags are set to become the next best thing in ticketing technology.

RFID stands for radio frequency identification. The tag is a piece of hardware that can be put into tickets or wristbands to collect real-time data from the ticket holder.

RFID ticketing technology is one of the most advanced ways of analyzing a customer's purchasing habits and behaviour. For example, if you are hosting a gig or an event, you can use the RFID wristband system to record attendance times, entry points and transactions made. This kind of information is invaluable when it comes to marketing strategies and customer services, whether it's in offering special offers on merchandise and food when sales are quiet or opening extra facilities when an area gets overcrowded.

Using the RFID Ticket System for Crowd Control

If you're hosting a large event such as a festival, RFID wristband technology is the perfect solution for effectively controlling a large number of customers. The RFID bracelet can be loaded with tickets and scanned upon entry, and the user can even load the wristband with cash and card details, eliminating the need to carry cash or make lengthy card payments.

Product Promotion and the RFID Ticket System

There are all sorts of innovative ways the RFID bracelet for events can be implemented to create a PR buzz. Recent examples have looked at social media links, giving event visitors the chance to upload playlists, photo booth photos and tweets via their RFID bracelet.

If you're looking to take your business to the next level at the forefront of technology, the RFID system is certain to unlock the potential.

Tickets with Speed & Functionality

If you've ever attempted to get tickets to see a popular musician, or you've tried to attend a sought-after event, you'll know that time is of the essence when it comes to snapping up one of the precious golden tickets.

Gone are the days of queuing in line with our sleeping bags and tents to get to the front of the queue on sale day, now we are a nation online, and it pays to have good tech that'll deal with online ticketing quickly and efficiently.

With companies offering modern solutions to buying, hot tickets are more accessible to anyone that invests in reliable technology and can pass through the purchase process easily. Mobile ticketing is one of the latest trends in the tale, giving users the chance to purchase tickets wherever they are, so you can conveniently log on and secure your tickets as soon as they are released.

Offering Quick Platforms to Cope with Demand

Speed in online ticketing software is also the best investment a company can make. Provide a quick, and user-friendly online ticketing service and your customers will be able to buy their tickets quickly and not be left out in the cold when it comes to their favourite events.

Investing in reliable tech that will cope with a sudden influx of online ticket sales is crucial to companies that are selling popular events. Businesses should also invest in the checkout process, to make sure it is as straightforward as possible, giving every customer a fair chance to buy that all-important online ticket.

Event Ticketing & Reservations Software

To create a ticketing and reservations system that is traveller-centric, the software must be cloud-based and include features such as integrated access controls, event management controls, multi-channel distribution capabilities, and a robust reporting suite. Additionally, the system must provide a customer-facing ticket sales page, inventory controls, invoicing, financial accountability, and the ability to link necessary transportation components for the event.

To ensure ease of use, the system should have an intuitive interface, and marketing tools to keep customers engaged and allow clients to access all ticket sales and donation information in one place. The software must also seamlessly integrate with existing box office and transit operations via APIs.

The system should accommodate orders taken by phone, fax, mail, box office, and the Internet. It should support reserved seating, and general admission seating, and handle events with a combination of both. It should easily program seating charts and handle season tickets or subscription needs.

To enhance customer relationships, the software should offer a suite of customer reports, email marketing tools, customer history tracking, and other CRM tools to help the organization understand and grow its traveller-centric base. The system should also include a variety of reporting tools that allow authorized users to separate data by event, event type, event category, method of payment, order type, cashier, event date range, and transaction date range.

Finally, the system should support real-time barcode, QR code and RFID scanning for ticket validation and attendance reporting. It should seamlessly integrate ticket purchasing into the organization's website, with a fully customized look and feel to match the existing website. A graphical active map selection engine with a calendar-driven graphical user interface, providing a colour-coded graphical seating or placement display, should also be included.

E-Tickets and Print Tickets Scanning

With a Traveller-centric ticketing system, you can forward an e-boarding pass by email, which clients can print at home, or use directly from their smartphone (all platforms are supported). E-Tickets and Print Tickets Scanning, no paper needed! In short, clients can now bypass the ticket office and go directly to your location on their date of departure.

Their boarding pass (either printed or on their smartphone) can be scanned by your employees both at the boarding gate as well as on board the train. Your staff can be equipped with a hand scanner, which is linked to your Traveller-centric central reservation system.

When scanned, the boarding pass will be validated and the passenger's name added to the "virtual" list of passengers travelling on that train.

This is a more efficient and reliable way of updating the passenger list. It also means that other departments can have access to real-time information. Staff will know, immediately, how many seats are still available on the train (for any stand-by passengers), or if any ticket holders are missing (announcements can be made).

Having a wireless system means that tickets can be validated on board, en route, anywhere and at any time. You can also set up wireless ticket printers to allow staff to make reservations, and print and scan wirelessly, anywhere, anytime.

Waiting in line and carrying cash is now outdated. Thanks to mobile ticketing, customers can now purchase a ticket anywhere in the world, if they have an internet connection and a smartphone.

Mobile ticketing gives customers the ability to purchase tickets straight from their smartphones, which not only saves them time and money, it saves resources too.

As well as using it to purchase their tickets, customers can use mobile ticketing to display any tickets they have purchased. This reduces paper usage and speeds up the boarding process for transport companies, and the turnaround time for hotels, restaurants and many more businesses that choose to implement mobile ticketing software.

One of the greatest features of mobile ticketing is its ability to be integrated into your business quickly. A new fare collection structure will usually take weeks or even months to implement, but mobile ticketing technology can often be incorporated into a business in a matter of days.

Mobile ticketing technology is the most convenient way to buy your travel, whether it's for your weekly train ticket to work, a bus ride at the weekend, or a connecting flight during a backpacking tour across the world. You can use mobile ticketing anywhere in the world, as long as you have a smartphone and an internet connection, and this is revolutionizing the way we purchase tickets and travel.

Mobile ticketing software has not only transformed the way we buy our transport tickets, but it is also beginning to change the way we carry our tickets. With mobile ticketing solutions, you can now store transport tickets, boarding passes and travel cards on your smartphone, making your journeys easier than ever before.

The 21st-century mobile ticketing platform is a huge time saver, not only in eliminating the need to queue to purchase tickets but in the swift movement of passengers through a transport hub. Innovative scanning software allows you to swipe your mobile tickets from your phone, letting you move through barriers and checkpoints quicker than ever before.

Recent studies have indicated that mobile ticketing, where a customer buys a bus ticket on their mobile phone, reduces passenger boarding times by many seconds per passenger.

This is typical because most bus and ferry services particularly city buses and fast ferry type of operations require passengers to have the exact fare at the point of boarding or to purchase a ticket from the appropriate kiosks or ticketing machines.

Choices available for mobile ticketing typically depend upon customers downloading the appropriate Apple or Android app to their smartphone. This enables customers to then purchase tickets; including daily, weekly and monthly tickets which are then paid for using a credit or debit card.

A virtual ticket can then be stored on the passenger's phone and shown to the driver when boarding the bus and /or scanned as part of a boarding or departure control system.

As an adjunct, it should allow booking, seat selection, reservations across multiple lines, etc. and provides ticket purchase, display and inspection together with back-end infrastructure for secure payments, ticket management, customer service, reporting and real-time analytics to operate as a mobile ticketing solution.

Barcode ticketing and scanning are essential to the security of any company that uses ticketing, whether it be mobile ticketing for transport or online ticketing for events.

The Barcode Scanner

A barcode scanner is a simple device that is used at the point of entry to a ticketed event or venue and can be used in multiple locations if necessary. When a ticket is scanned using the barcode ticket scanner, the barcode is checked and verified, and real-time information is given as to the validity of the ticket.

Ticket Barcode Verification

Barcode scanner solutions are your company's safeguard against fraudulent and duplicated tickets. If your staff member uses the ticket barcode scanner to read a duplicated ticket, he or she will be immediately notified and will be given all the necessary information regarding the duplication, from the original point of purchase and the purchaser's name to the time the ticket was originally scanned. Ticket barcode verification is essential for venues and events that suffer from fraudulent ticket activity.

Barcode Scanner Support

Any PC-based fixed/mobile computer/iPhone, etc., with a built-in or attached scanner which will access the web via any onboard Wi-Fi / Internet-connected system on the ferry, bus or your land-based ticket office.

Whats the Benefit of Using BarCodes?

The benefits of using BarCodes and QR codes or RFID for ticket solutions and automated data collection are very simple: speed and accuracy. Time after time, it has been proven that entering BarCode data is at least 100 times faster and more accurate than traditional manual keyboard entry, which translates into a dramatic increase in efficiency and productivity for any operation.

Run Your Business More Efficiently

The barcode ticket system also helps speed up the process of entry when it comes to checking tickets. Staff members are given validation within seconds, which aids the continuous movement of traffic even at busy venues. A barcode ticket scanner is also a mobile unit, which allows you to increase the points of entry to a venue, as you won't have to install each entry point with permanent and bulky hardware.

The barcode ticketing software works online, usually via Wi-Fi, but if there is limited internet access within your operating ground, you can enable each ticket barcode scanner with a sim that allows mobile internet access.

Smartwatch Tickets or Wearable Technology.

The design and inclusion of smart wearable technology in a smart city reservation system have revolutionized the way we interact with tickets and access various services. One of the key components of this system is the integration of smartwatch tickets and other wearable technologies, similar to mobile ticketing. This advancement allows a diverse range of tickets, such as travel passes, event tickets, and festival tickets, to be conveniently delivered to your smartphone and now, also to your smartwatch.

As the number of smartwatch users continues to grow, companies across different industries are recognizing the potential of offering services through this technology. Whether it's travel companies streamlining the ticketing process or music festival organizers enhancing the overall experience, businesses are actively embracing smartwatch ticket services. By doing so, they aim to make it even more convenient for consumers to manage their tickets and enjoy seamless access to various events and services.

The introduction of smartwatch ticketing eliminates the hassles associated with traditional ticket management. Users no longer need to worry about keeping physical tickets safe or printing them out. The smartwatch serves as a reliable and easily accessible repository for all their tickets. Furthermore, concerns regarding smartphone battery life or signal strength, which could impact ticket retention and usability, are eliminated. Wearable technology tickets ensure that the ticketing process is simple, convenient, and free from potential disruptions.

What was once perceived as a modern replacement for paper tickets has now evolved into an interactive and comprehensive service. Digital ticketing has embraced an array of interactive features and is poised to continue evolving in the future. Further advancements are anticipated, promising to deliver a more enriched and fulfilling experience for the modern retail customer.

In addition to the core ticketing functionality, smartwatch technology opens up opportunities for additional features and integrations within the smart city reservation system. For instance, wearable devices can provide real-time updates and notifications about event details, venue changes, or time-sensitive information. Users can receive reminders or alerts directly on their smartwatches, ensuring they stay informed and prepared.

Moreover, smartwatches offer the potential for personalized recommendations and tailored experiences. By leveraging user data and preferences, the reservation system can suggest relevant events, activities, or services that align with individual interests. This customization enhances the overall customer experience and promotes engagement with the smart city ecosystem.

The adoption of smartwatch technology within the smart city reservation system also paves the way for seamless access to various facilities and services beyond ticketing. Users can utilize their smartwatches to access public transportation systems, gain entry to secure areas or make cashless payments within the city. This consolidation of functionalities into a single wearable device streamlines daily interactions, reduces the need for multiple physical cards or tickets, and enhances overall convenience for residents and visitors alike.

As smart cities continue to evolve, the design and inclusion of smart wearable technology in reservation systems play a pivotal role in creating a connected and user-centric urban environment. The integration of smartwatch tickets and other wearable technologies offers numerous benefits, including convenience, reliability, enhanced experiences, and expanded functionalities. With ongoing advancements and innovations in this field, the future promises even greater integration of wearable technology, enabling residents and visitors to enjoy seamless access to a multitude of services and experiences within the smart city ecosystem.

Transport and the City

In the evolving landscape of urban mobility, the efficiency and convenience of transportation systems have become critical for the residents of smart cities. The advent of mobile ticketing technology presents an opportunity to address the strain on city transport systems and revolutionize the way people move within urban areas. By leveraging mobile ticketing solutions, smart cities can empower travellers to navigate seamlessly, eliminate lengthy queues, access real-time information, and experience stress-free transport. This design recommendation explores the wide-ranging potential of mobile ticketing technology, envisioning a comprehensive and traveller-centric reservation system for smart cities.

1. Enhanced Mobility and Freedom: A fundamental objective of a smart city's transportation system is to provide travellers with the freedom to move effortlessly throughout the city. A mobile ticketing solution should enable passengers to access various modes of transport seamlessly. Beyond traditional train and subway tickets, the system should encompass cab booking, bus fare payment, bike rentals, and even real-time updates on transport delays. This holistic approach ensures travellers have a unified platform to manage their entire journey, regardless of the mode of transportation.

2. Seamlessness and Convenience: The mobile ticketing system should prioritize a seamless user experience. Travellers should be able to perform all necessary actions, from purchasing tickets to accessing real-time information, with ease and minimal effort. A user-friendly mobile application should be developed, providing a centralized hub for all travel-related activities. By integrating various services and offering a single point of access, the system reduces waiting times, eliminates the need for physical tickets or cash, and streamlines the overall travel experience.

3. Real-time Information and Updates: A critical aspect of a traveller-centric mobile ticketing system is the provision of up-to-date information. By leveraging the power of data and connectivity, the system should deliver real-time updates on routes, schedules, delays, and alternative transportation options. This empowers travellers to make informed decisions and adapt their plans accordingly. The mobile application should feature live maps, predictive analytics, and personalized notifications to keep users well-informed throughout their journey.

4. Integration and Interoperability: To maximize the benefits of a mobile ticketing system, seamless integration with existing transportation infrastructure and services is essential. Collaboration with transport operators, taxi services, bike-sharing platforms, and other stakeholders should be established to create an interconnected network. The mobile ticketing system should support interoperability, allowing travellers to seamlessly transition between different modes of transport using a single digital ticket or payment method. This integration promotes the adoption of the system by both travellers and service providers.

5. Security and Privacy: To ensure widespread acceptance and trust, the mobile ticketing system must prioritize security and privacy. Robust encryption techniques and authentication mechanisms should be implemented to safeguard user data and payment information. Compliance with relevant privacy regulations and standards should be adhered to strictly. By establishing a secure foundation, the system can encourage travellers to embrace the convenience of mobile ticketing without concerns about their personal information.

6. User Feedback and Continuous Improvement: To maintain a traveller-centric approach, it is crucial to gather user feedback

and continuously improve the mobile ticketing system. The development team should actively engage with travellers to understand their needs, pain points, and suggestions for enhancement. User feedback mechanisms, such as ratings, reviews, and surveys, should be incorporated into the mobile application. Regular updates and feature additions based on user input will ensure the system evolves to meet the dynamic demands of smart city travellers.

A traveller-centric mobile ticketing system holds tremendous potential to transform the way people navigate smart cities. By embracing mobile ticketing technology, smart cities can offer their residents seamless mobility, reduced waiting times, cashless transactions, and real-time information. The recommended design approach emphasizes a comprehensive, integrated, and user-friendly system that empowers travellers

Harmonizing Technology and Urban Life: Digital Features for a Smarter Cityscape

The future of account-based ticketing and payments in making major cities "smart cities" is the ability to provide a framework that allows multiple organizations to link their cards or apps into a single, seamless system.

For example, activity providers, major venues and transit providers can integrate to create combined access, travel and in-venue payment experience. This would allow smartcards, membership cards and other payment methods to be utilized across the city not only for transit but for entrance into venues, book activities, and purchase from retailers all able to link up to the same system and utilize the same access and payment system.

The shift to open payments for online booking, reservations, ticketing and payments, like every other major technological change, has its own unique set of challenges and complications. One of the first issues to be considered is whether customers in a specific regional market have sufficient adoption rates of contactless EMV payment cards and NFC devices to benefit from an open payment scheme

The advantage of using a Traveller-centric system is that it should support the older barcode and paper ticket technology and also at the same time utilize the modern mobile, smartcard account-based ticketing and open payments.

A further consideration for transport operators, in particular, is how to transition to open payments. With a Traveller-centric system, a well-managed transition to an open payment and account-based solution would include consideration at the initial design stage to allow for the open scheme to coexist alongside the existing close ticketing scheme using the system as the bridge.

It is becoming increasingly clear, that the entire transit industry and smart city tourist ecosystems are part of a shift to enable more cost-efficient and easier ways for passengers to make reservations, issue tickets and also allow operators to process fare collections.

The following are suggestions that would apply to functionality in a Smart City Traveller-centric software system.

Point of Sale Cash Register Functions

Point of Sale Cash Register Functions is a standard add-on to any kiosk to provide 'Cash Register' functions for online sales staff and admin.

Quick and Easy Point of Sale Processing – Help customers at the point of sale, ring up sales online, add discounts, look up items, find customers and process payments simply and quickly.

Inventory Management – Eliminate time-consuming paper-based tracking, reduce errors and remember to re-order stock when it's running low instead of when you run out.

Customer Management – Enhance customer service and relationships by enabling you to access purchase histories and assign automatic discounts to your preferred customers.

Access Management – Assign employees different levels of access to help protect sensitive information and manage employees more effectively, so you don't have to be in-store all the time.

Reporting – Boost your business planning capabilities so you can stay on top of your business better.

Content Management

Most website designers today are choosing a responsive design. Not only because it's cheaper and easier, but because it's so much more efficient to create one design that adjusts to different screen sizes than to create many designs optimized for all the different phones that exist now, as well as all of the new phones and devices that will come out in the future.

Here are the essential elements:

Web Hosting: You'll need a web hosting service that provides server space to store your website files and a database to store your CMS data.

Server Environment: Ensure your hosting environment supports the necessary server-side technologies for your chosen CMS. Common requirements include PHP, Python, or Node.js, along with the required versions.

Database Management System: Most CMS platforms rely on a database to store content, user information, and other data. Popular choices include MySQL, PostgreSQL, or SQLite. Ensure that your hosting environment supports the database system required by your CMS.

Domain Name: Register a domain name for your website to make it accessible to users. Choose a memorable and relevant domain name that aligns with your brand or website's purpose.

CMS Software: Select a CMS platform that suits your needs. Popular options include WordPress, Joomla, Drupal, and many others. Each CMS has its own installation and setup process, so follow the documentation provided by the CMS platform you choose.

Software Dependencies: Verify that your hosting environment meets the CMS's software requirements. This may include specific versions of PHP, database extensions, libraries, or server modules.

Secure Connection (SSL): Implement a Secure Sockets Layer (SSL) certificate to enable HTTPS encryption for secure communication between your website and its visitors. It helps protect sensitive user information and enhances trust.

Themes and Templates: Consider choosing or creating a theme or template for your CMS to define the visual appearance of your website. Many CMS platforms offer a wide range of free and premium themes that you can customize to match your branding.

Plugins and Extensions: Explore the available plugins or extensions for your chosen CMS to extend its functionality. These can include features such as SEO optimization, e-commerce capabilities, contact forms, social media integration, and more.

User Roles and Permissions: Determine the user roles and permissions required for managing your website. Most CMS platforms offer the ability to assign roles like administrators, editors, authors, and contributors with varying levels of access and capabilities.

Backup and Security: Implement a regular backup system to ensure your CMS data is protected. Additionally, utilize security measures like strong passwords, regular software updates, and security plugins to safeguard your website from vulnerabilities and potential attacks.

Remember to consult the specific documentation and guidelines provided by your chosen CMS platform for detailed instructions on installation, configuration, and customization.

Integrated Coupon & Promotions Engine

Consideration should be given to integrating a Coupon & Promotions Engine. Such a system helps merchants build customer loyalty and promote increased traffic to your Web sites.

The coupon system features an immediate discount at the time of sale, so your customer receives immediate gratification!

Utilizing a simple coupon code that you launch to existing customers via email, your website descriptions, Newsletters, online brochures and to prospective customers via Banner Ads, this is an effective and affordable way to Fuel Your Sales!

With an integrated Coupon Promotions Engine, the admin can pre-determine the special offer and when your customer comes to your Web site to make a purchase, they enter the code you have supplied and your special offer is redeemed right then and there!

The systems should recognize the discount and coupon validity period you have pre-programmed and will apply that approved discount instantly when your customer clicks your "Buy Now or Order" buttons.

Your customers save money when making a reservation with your reservations software by joining your company's rewards program. This integrated coupons and promotion program offers coupons, promo codes, rewards points and other attractive features for your customers.

It is preferable to build a Self-Managed Coupon Management System with complete backend access and control over every aspect of your coupons including distribution, promotion and redemption:

-Create Targeted Coupons, Deals & Points for Activities from the unified dashboard.

-Distribute Offers to customer groups through multiple channels viz. Website, Email, Mobile apps and Social networks.

-Access customer Insights & Manage points, activities, customers and redemption.

Coupons are capable of supporting multiple rules, ensuring the most comprehensive and flexible coupon eCommerce solution for the marketing success of your online business.

Credit Card Gateways Controller

Build a system that supports many credit card gateways and supports the Address Verification System.

In a reservation system, a credit card gateway controller is responsible for handling credit card transactions and facilitating the payment process. It acts as a bridge between the reservation system and the payment gateway, which is a service that securely processes credit card payments.

The credit card gateway controller performs the following key functions:

1. Payment Authorization: When a customer makes a reservation and chooses to pay by credit card, the credit card gateway controller interacts with the payment gateway to authorize the payment. It sends the relevant payment details (credit card number, expiration date, CVV, etc.) to the

payment gateway for verification and approval.

2. Security and Encryption: The credit card gateway controller ensures that all sensitive payment information is transmitted securely. It uses encryption protocols (such as SSL/TLS) to protect the data during transmission between the reservation system and the payment gateway. It also adheres to industry security standards, such as Payment Card Industry Data Security Standard (PCI DSS), to maintain the security of credit card transactions.

3. Transaction Logging: The credit card gateway controller logs transaction details for auditing and reconciliation purposes. It captures important information, including the transaction amount, timestamp, payment status, and any error messages received from the payment gateway. These logs can be used for troubleshooting, financial reporting, or resolving payment-related issues.

4. Payment Response Handling: Once the payment gateway processes the credit card transaction, it sends a response back to the credit card gateway controller. The controller interprets the response, determines whether the payment was successful or declined, and updates the reservation system accordingly. It may also trigger any necessary actions, such as sending confirmation emails or updating inventory availability.

5. Error Handling and Exception Handling: In case of errors or exceptions during the payment process, the credit card gateway controller handles them appropriately. It communicates error messages or declined transaction notifications to the reservation system, which can then inform the customer or take necessary actions, such as offering alternative payment methods.

6. Integration with Reservation System: The credit card gateway

controller integrates with the reservation system to exchange relevant information. It receives reservation details, such as customer information, reservation amount, and booking reference, from the reservation system. It also provides status updates and transaction details back to the reservation system for record-keeping and order management purposes.

Overall, the credit card gateway controller plays a crucial role in securely processing credit card payments within a reservation system, ensuring smooth transactions and maintaining the confidentiality and integrity of sensitive payment data.

Also be aware that if you are using one of these remote-hosted ASP or CGI-style reservation systems, they may not be PCI compliant.

As must also be considered, who is responsible for the security of their shared databases? Is your customer data secure? Who has access to it?

Customer Relationship Management CRM

A CRM should enable tourism, transit and hospitality businesses to effectively manage their enquiries, reservations, loyalty rewards, coupon promotions, secure transactions, newsletters, email marketing and so much more.

A CRM typically includes a customer profile section that is shared between the entire system and stores every reservation, event booking, tour, trip, note and transaction forever.

When a repeat customer makes a new reservation, the information from their profile is displayed and automatically loaded into the new reservation. A Customer Loyalty Reward should be available also.

The customer profile information is kept separate from reservation history, so when a customer books a few times, it stores only one customer profile record, with the entire reservation records linked to it. All the information is stored in the database and made accessible to all features.

1. Provide your organization with a unified customer data view for enhanced customer service and customer marketing intelligence.
2. Manage preferences, related passengers, order history, frequent traveller programs, membership levels and more.
3. Manage travel partners, consortia, groups and other organizations within a unified data environment. Streamline and improve business process flows with an integrated workflow engine.
4. Intelligently market to your customers and prospects using customer data.

Allow your partners to build advanced integration with your product data using an integrated XML API

Affiliate Networks

It is recommended you consider a fully integrated system that allows you to set up a variety of commission and payment-related access points for your travel agents and third-party resellers of your products.

Using an affiliate network in a booking and reservation smart city system can be a strategic decision depending on your specific circumstances and goals. Here are some factors to consider when evaluating the usefulness and worthiness of an affiliate network for your smart city system:

1. Access to a wider range of options: An affiliate network can provide access to a broader inventory of hotels, accommodations, transportation services, and other offerings. This can enhance the user experience by providing more choices and increasing the likelihood of finding suitable options.
2. Monetization opportunities: By partnering with an affiliate network, you can earn commission or referral fees for each successful booking made through your system. This can

create an additional revenue stream and potentially offset the costs associated with developing and maintaining the smart city system.

3. Reduced development and maintenance effort: Integrating with an affiliate network can save you the time and effort required to individually establish relationships with multiple hotels, transportation providers, and other relevant businesses. The network may already have existing integrations and APIs that simplify the implementation process.

4. Trust and credibility: Partnering with established and reputable affiliate networks can lend credibility to your smart city system. Users may feel more confident booking through your platform if they recognize and trust the affiliate network's brand.

5. Potential downsides: There are some potential drawbacks to consider. Using an affiliate network means relying on a third party for inventory, and you may not have full control over pricing, availability, or customer support. Additionally, you may face competition from other systems that offer similar affiliate partnerships.

Ultimately, whether using an affiliate network is worth it depends on your specific goals, resources, and the nature of your smart city system. It's important to carefully evaluate the potential benefits and drawbacks, consider the specific needs of your target users, and conduct a cost-benefit analysis to make an informed decision.

Unified Customer View

As a Smart City, whether you are an independent organisation within that entity or group, or chain, you can improve your customer relationships and market more effectively to them through a unified customer view.

Capture preferences and use them in the reservation and room assignment process. Provide your reservations specialists and call centre agents with key customer data, travel preferences, related customers, membership, and past stay information. Offers and specials are stored with customer profiles, providing enhanced access and response capabilities.

Instant Confirmation – Immediately "Close the Deal"

The system must generate instant confirmation for reservations, modifications and cancellations, which is automatically sent to the customer's email, administration, hotel/tour operator and travel agents. Instant confirmations enable travel agents to immediately "close the sale" thereby reducing the risk of guests' shopping around, besides reducing expenses on fax or phone confirmations of all reservation activities.

Empower Your Website

Empowers your website, as a virtual office, to capture reservation enquiries. Website visitors have access to your rates and availability information as will all authorized travel agents, thereby encouraging them to make reservations immediately online.

Your associated travel agents do not need to manually maintain all their contracted rates and inventory, as the latest update is available in the system and can be viewed by any designated reservation staff, at any time, in a real-time manner (online). Thus, reservation inquiries can be responded to promptly, cost effectively while increasing your reservation volumes.

Put Your Booking Icon on Your Resellers Desktop Easy access equals more sales! Place your booking ICON right on the reseller's desktop. Your products are right at their fingertips when it matters most – during the sales process.

Dynamic Waitlist

A dynamic waitlist program is a powerful tool that can greatly enhance the efficiency and effectiveness of waitlist management in various contexts. Whether it is used in a restaurant, a hotel, a university, or any other organization that deals with waitlists, this program offers numerous benefits that can streamline operations and improve customer satisfaction.

One key advantage of a dynamic waitlist program is its ability to automate the process of managing waitlists. Traditionally, managing a waitlist involved manual entry, constant monitoring, and frequent updates. This not only consumed valuable time and resources but also increased the chances of errors or oversights. With a dynamic waitlist program, however, the entire process is automated. Customers can join the waitlist digitally, and the program can automatically send notifications and updates regarding their status, estimated wait times, and any available slots. This automation significantly reduces human error and ensures a smooth and efficient waitlist management system.

Another valuable feature of a dynamic waitlist program is its ability to provide real-time data and analytics. By tracking customer preferences, patterns, and behaviour, the program can generate insightful reports and analytics that can help businesses make informed decisions. For instance, it can identify peak hours or popular time slots, allowing businesses to optimize their operations accordingly. It can also track customer satisfaction levels and feedback, enabling organizations to continuously improve their services and tailor their offerings to meet customer demands.

Furthermore, a dynamic waitlist program can enhance the overall customer experience. With automated notifications and updates, customers no longer have to physically wait in line or repeatedly check for availability. They can go about their other activities and receive timely alerts when their turn is approaching. This convenience not only saves time but also enhances customer satisfaction and loyalty. Additionally, the program can offer personalized experiences by collecting customer data and preferences, allowing businesses to cater to individual needs and provide tailored recommendations.

In conclusion, a dynamic waitlist program is a valuable tool that revolutionizes waitlist management by automating the process, providing real-time data and analytics, and enhancing the customer experience. By leveraging technology and streamlining operations, organizations can optimize their resources, improve efficiency, and deliver exceptional customer service. Whether it is reducing wait times, minimizing errors, or gaining valuable insights, a dynamic waitlist program offers numerous advantages that can drive success in various industries.

Dynamic Reservation Content

Are you interested in serving dynamic content that is relevant to the time and location of the consumer?

For example, if a registered client opens the transit/tour application two weeks before a trip/tour, they may want to change their trip/tour.

Two days before, they may want to change their seat, and two hours before, they probably want to access their ticket/s to reprint/display.

Times that suit your business can be set up in a rules engine they then become effective as your clients log in to their accounts.

Depending upon the time before departure, and after they log in, they are sent directly to the relevant section according to the time/date and rule set up.

Digital Cart Parking

Surveys have shown that approximately (61%) of shoppers changed their minds and discarded their checkout contents and (47%) wanted to save items for later purchases but had no option to do so.

Consider the development and addition of some form of Digital Cart Parking, whereby your potential purchaser and guests may park their digital cart checkout for up to 30 days merely by choosing that option.

Next time the guest visits your website they are reminded that their parked checkout is available.

Reminder notices and other up-selling techniques are available for converting that parked reservation into a sale.

The actual product/room/tour or items are not pulled out of inventory until the reservation, purchase or checkout process is completed.

Event Calendar

Add an Event calendar for single events, recurring events and floating events plus multiple categories, mouse-over display, etc.

Providing an easy-to-navigate point-and-click interface that allows visitors to your website to quickly know what Tour and/or Transit events are planned.

Ensure its input is automated, making it a quick, efficient solution for displaying to your visitors, information related to specific times of the month and year.

Single events, recurring events and floating events:

Automatically adds all events from reservation points set up as you add them.

Such as flexible event types that occur on a specific date; events that repeat daily, weekly, monthly or annually; floating events, which occur on specific days etc.

Virtually unlimited user-definable categories and colours to separate events:

Calendar Display Mode

Create, maintain and assign multiple levels of categories and selections to events. Then, using the filter system, you can choose to selectively display categories such as Cruises, Shuttle, Kayak, Routes and any other category you should ever need.

Mouse-over and pop-up event details:

Hover the mouse pointer over an event and a pop-up will appear showing complete details about the event. The size, position, layout and options of the pop-ups are all customizable.

Rich event descriptions including font sizes/colours and images:

Easily customize colours, font sizes, calendar sizes and more by adjusting just one access point and having complete control over how the calendar looks and interacts with users!

Consider setting up "Fare Buckets" similar to the airline industry for Tou and Transit operations by creating stratified layers of fares, each with different rules, perks and prices.

Make it possible to create different price groups or tiers using tour items for the Tour or Transit modules.

Assign fare basis codes to the various "Fare buckets" of inventory available for sale on any given flight, trip or departure fares for first class, coach, business, etc.

You can use different inventories for different items.

An administrator can switch for each trip:

– "use common inventory for all items" (existing functionality)

or

-"Use separate inventory for each tour item".

The above can be used also with a Last Minute Pricing Deals feature.

Hotel Group Tours

In the traveller-centric system, it should be possible to offer not only individual hotel bookings but also to incorporate hotel group tours into the system. Administrators can modify the inventory specifically for these group tours, granting them flexibility and control over the available options.

Administrators should be empowered to select the rooms (tours) that will be included in the group tour, thereby generating inventory for all the rooms (tours) within that particular group. This enables administrators to curate a selection of rooms that best suits the requirements and preferences of the group tour.

When a customer utilizes the front-end system to make a booking, they will be able to check the availability of each room within the group tour period, as well as the overall availability of the group tour itself. This comprehensive check ensures that the customer has access to up-to-date information regarding the availability of both individual rooms and the group tour as a whole.

To proceed with booking Hotel Group tours within the system, the user needs to select the appropriate group tour from a dropdown box. Upon selection, a dedicated page displaying detailed information about the group tour will be opened, providing the user with a comprehensive overview of the tour's offerings.

At this stage, the user is required to enter the desired quantity of rooms and confirm their selection by clicking on the "OK" button. Subsequently, all the tours included in the group tour should be seamlessly added to the checkout process, ensuring a streamlined and efficient booking experience for the customer.

Upon successful completion of the booking, the inventory for both the group tour and all the individual rooms within the group will be automatically adjusted. This form of dynamic inventory management system ensures that the availability is accurately reflected, preventing overbooking and ensuring a smooth and reliable booking process for future customers.

Last Minute Pricing

Consider offering businesses a powerful tool to maximize revenue and attract customers through a Last-Minute Pricing Deals feature. This feature would allow businesses operating in the tourism industry, including tours, hotels, and transit companies, to set up additional costs or discounts based on the number of hours remaining before a trip.

A Last-Minute Pricing Deals feature goes beyond simple pricing adjustments. Consider intelligent rate pricing structures, capable of accommodating even the most intricate configurations. This flexibility enables businesses to tailor their pricing strategies to specific market conditions and optimize their revenue potential.

With the ability to support true last-minute rates, it empowers businesses to capitalize on the dynamic nature of the travel industry. As prices for travel services typically begin to decline approximately three weeks before departure, it becomes crucial for businesses to adjust their rates accordingly. The system simplifies this process by allowing for daily, and even multiple daily, price changes. This agility ensures that businesses stay competitive in a market where pricing fluctuations can make all the difference.

Furthermore, a Last-Minute Pricing Deals feature can seamlessly integrate with a Fare Bucket feature, providing businesses with enhanced control and precision over their pricing strategies. This integration allows businesses to allocate specific inventory or fare types to last-minute deals, ensuring optimal utilization and revenue generation.

While last-minute travel deals traditionally become more accessible as the departure date approaches, certain periods of the year may present less opportunity for such discounts. The system should recognise this and offers businesses the flexibility to modify prices and discounts for these specific periods. By leveraging the easily adjustable pricing capabilities of the software, businesses can manage and optimize their revenue during these periods effectively.

Also, enable businesses to reduce prices well in advance with Early Booking Bonuses. By offering incentives to customers who book their vacations ahead of time, businesses can secure bookings early on, optimize capacity utilization, and reward their loyal customers with discounted rates.

In summary, with intelligent rate pricing structures, support for true last-minute and early-bird rates, and seamless integration with the Fare Bucket feature, businesses can maximize revenue, adapt to market conditions, and deliver exceptional value to their customers. Whether it's capturing last-minute opportunities or encouraging early bookings, your Traveller-centric system must empower businesses to stay competitive and thrive in an ever-changing travel landscape.

Loyalty Rewards Points and Reward Programs

Traveller-centric systems can improve the mobility booking experience by offering personalized and priced seat availability, putting the power of choice directly in the hands of the customers. Gone are the days of generic offerings and rigid loyalty programs. With newer systems travellers should be able to tailor their shopping journey to their preferences, while enjoying dynamic "build your loyalty" options.

Provide users with greater choice and flexibility. Through rules-based management, customers should now earn and redeem rewards in a way that aligns with their individual needs and desires. By allocating different amounts of rewards, such as points, to various products, services, or fare bundles presented during the shopping process, users have full control over their loyalty programs.

Additionally, establish a multitude of user-controlled criteria to further customize their experience. This innovative approach, in conjunction with integrated features like "Fare Buckets," Coupons, "Bundles & Package Deals," and "Discount" programs, offers a truly unique and rewarding method of engaging with clients.

Why stop at personalized offerings and loyalty rewards? Provide the flexibility to bundle and unbundle products and services, enabling smart and adaptable price points throughout the promotion and purchase stages. Whether customers are seeking exclusive deals or looking to customize their travel experience, the system can store all the products and services purchased, ensuring optimization and relevance across all touch points. This comprehensive approach guarantees a seamless and satisfying shopping experience from start to finish.

One of the features should be a Loyalty Reward Points and Loyalty Rewards Programs module. By implementing this approach, administrators can effortlessly emulate the popular "miles" system utilized by the airline industry. Customers have the opportunity to earn points with every purchase they make, and these points can then be redeemed automatically for discounts or other merchandise. An intelligent loyalty program not only incentivizes repeat business but also strengthens customer engagement and drives sales.

Within a Loyalty Reward Points module, there should be unique features designed to enhance the customer experience. Earning points is made simple, as each product in the eCommerce, tour, hotel, rental, and transit modules must have a dedicated points field for easy assignment. Administrators can view and manually adjust the number of points associated with each user, providing granular control over the loyalty program. Customers can conveniently log into their accounts and access a summary of their available points, giving them full visibility and transparency.

Redeeming points should be equally straightforward within the system. Administrators can set a conversion rate between points and dollars or local currency, allowing customers to redeem their earned points for discounts on future purchases. For example, a 10% conversion rate means that customers can deduct $10 or equivalent from their next store purchase by redeeming 100 points. Alternatively, clients have the freedom to allocate points as they wish, providing them with additional flexibility and personalization. If the value of the points exceeds the order total, the system automatically utilizes the appropriate number of points, while the remaining points remain in the customer's account for future use.

Consider expanding beyond mere points accumulation and redemption. Customers can earn points not only through purchases but also through various actions, incentivizing engagement and rewarding customers for their loyalty. For instance, customers could earn points based on a conversion rate, such as 1 point for every dollar spent. This conversion rate can be customized at the category or product level, allowing businesses to strategically promote specific products and further encourage customer purchases. Points earned are prominently displayed on the product page and the cart/checkout page, ensuring transparency and motivating customers to take advantage of their rewards.

To facilitate efficient management of customer points, you should provide a user-friendly interface where administrators can quickly update a customer's points balance. Any changes made to a customer's points balance are logged and prominently displayed on the customer's account page, allowing for easy tracking and reference. Furthermore, ensure it offers a comprehensive range of reports, including sales reports, coupon reports, accrued points reports, points used reports, and more, enabling management to gain valuable insights into their loyalty programs and customer engagement.

In summary, with personalized seat availability and dynamic loyalty options, customers have unparalleled control and customization at their fingertips. The loyalty module empowers users to tailor their rewards based on specific criteria, while bundled products, smart pricing, and comprehensive touchpoint optimization enhance the overall shopping experience. A Loyalty Reward Points and Loyalty Rewards Programs module further incentivize customer loyalty, allowing for seamless points accumulation, redemption, and flexible point allocation.

Mobile Reservation Applications

A traveller-centric system must offer advanced reservation capabilities to customers seeking information and reservations, with applications specifically designed for those using iOS and Android devices. Understanding that travellers lead active lifestyles, and require enhanced mobile capabilities to accommodate their on-the-go needs, makes it easier than ever for them to make reservations anywhere, anytime, right from their mobile devices.

With the proposed system, customers must have the flexibility to make reservations using an internet browser or your dedicated application. They can conveniently access information about availability, pricing, and booking options, all from the palm of their hand. Whether they prefer to use their mobile device, phone, PDA, or any other compatible device, the system should also support touchscreen templates that are well-suited for various public venues such as point-of-sale (POS), point-of-information (POI), point-of-service, kiosk information systems, and office control.

Newsletter Software

When it comes to effectively communicating with your customers and keeping them informed about your latest offerings, consider utilizing integrated newsletter software instead of relying on third-party programs. By doing so, you can maintain confidentiality while seamlessly updating your customers about sales promotions, "Hot Deals," or any other new announcements through periodic mailings or online newsletters.

Growing your business requires effectively conveying the benefits of your products or services to your customers. While traditional advertising methods like billboards, flyers, and television ads can be effective within a city, it's essential to incorporate emails into your advertising mix.

Email marketing offers numerous advantages, serving as an electronic and efficient alternative to direct mail. By customizing your email newsletters with engaging content, relevant images, and important links, you can achieve your email marketing goals effectively. With familiar WYSIWYG text formatting buttons and easy personalization features, you can create professional emails more efficiently.

Add a newsletter section to the software that is specifically designed to streamline your email communication. It allows you to send emails to multiple contacts from your client database, efficiently manage un-subscribes, and run newsletters seamlessly. By keeping in constant touch with your customers, you can ensure your company remains top-of-mind and nurtures valuable relationships with your most important stakeholders.

Empower your business with efficient and effective email marketing, ensuring your customers receive timely updates and remain engaged with your brand.

Upsell Merchandising

Implement a merchandising feature that enables the creation of unlimited related links between products that are complementary or similar. This feature will allow customers to easily access and select additional items of value on the same page as the main product.

By using this feature, when a customer chooses a trip ticket, room, tour, or product, related complementary products will be displayed on the same page. This way, the buyer can select additional products without the need to navigate through the website or forget to buy them.

The benefit of this feature is that it will enable a traveller-centric system to increase sales by offering more products to customers.

Partial Payments & Deposits

Consider the following design requirement for a "Deposit/ Remaining" feature, to include the following functionalities:

1. Ability to set a minimum deposit value (in percentage or USD) for each tour, trip, room, product, or rental in the admin area.
2. The ability for customers to enter a deposit for each booked item, which can be either X-percent or more than X-percent (if the administrator has set a minimum deposit value for the item in percentage) or X-amount or more than X-amount (if the administrator has set a minimum deposit value for the item in USD/selected currency).
3. Changes in the calculation of order subtotal, which will be the sum of all deposit values for each item in the order.

4. Display of deposit/remaining values on checkout, thank you pages, emails, and the admin area for the selected order.
5. The ability for both customers and administrators to pay the remaining amount for each order via the account's personal orders page for customers and the orders -> list orders -> selected order page for administrators.
6. Once the remaining amount is paid, the system will change the order status to "Remaining paid" and display the remaining payment date on the order details page in the admin area.

PCI Compliance

To ensure the safety of your customer's credit card and data, it is important to comply with the latest industry standards set by the Payment Card Industry Security Standards Council (PCI SSC). This includes ensuring that your software is PCI compliant and utilizes "strong" encryption for credit card numbers if they are stored in your database. Additionally, it is important not to store swiped data from any credit card unless specifically selected to do so and to support SSL, strong encryption, and other security measures when passing credit card numbers through your online booking engine or desktop applications.

Furthermore, security codes should never be stored or transferred in any database, as they are only meant for imminent transactions. Full card numbers should not be printed on invoices, emails, or other forms of communication, and if full credit card numbers are stored, they should only be accessed through an encrypted username and password at the top administration level.

To ensure that your customers are protected, it is important to support an "auto-logoff" feature, which automatically logs customers off after a period of inactivity, typically 15 minutes. It is also important to store credit card information in a PCI-compliant environment for systems that take credit card numbers to secure reservations.

It is important to note that remote-hosted ASP or CGI-style reservation systems may not be PCI compliant, so it is important to verify the security of any shared databases and ensure that customer data is secure and access is restricted only to those who need it. By following these industry standards, you can help protect your customers' credit cards and data and build their trust in your business.

Ticket Wallet

Consider a "print at home" feature in modern ticketing systems as a convenient way for customers to receive their purchased tickets without having to wait in long lines or worry about misplacing physical tickets. This feature offers a variety of options for customers, including the choice to receive a traditional ticket in the mail, pick up their tickets at an outlet or embarkation point, or simply print their tickets at home.

When a customer selects the print-at-home option, they receive an Adobe Acrobat PDF file or QR code that contains all the details of their purchase. This PDF file or QR code acts as their ticket, containing a unique encrypted barcode that allows for the detection of counterfeit tickets and validates entry to the tours, seats, or events.

Upon arrival at the venue, the physical paper ticket or QR code on a mobile device is passed under an optical scanner that reads the barcode in real time. The ticketing system then verifies the admission information, allowing for a quick and efficient admission process. This system also ensures that each ticket is valid and unique, preventing any fraudulent activity.

The use of barcode and QR code technology has greatly improved the ticketing process, making it more secure, efficient, and convenient for both customers and venues. With the print-at-home option, customers can avoid the hassle of waiting in lines or risking lost tickets while venue operators benefit from a more streamlined and secure admission process.

Real-Time Sales Reports

Staying informed and connected with your ticket sales is crucial for any organization that hosts events, shows, or performances. One effective way to achieve this is through real-time ticketing reports. By utilizing these reports, you can access up-to-the-minute data on your ticket sales, enabling you to make informed decisions and take timely action.

To set up a comprehensive reporting system, you should consider creating a variety of reports that cater to the specific needs of your organization. These reports can include daily ticket sales reports that provide a detailed overview of the tickets sold daily. You can also generate sales by event reports that allow you to compare the sales of different events and evaluate their popularity.

Customer reports can provide valuable insights into the demographics and preferences of your ticket buyers. You can gather information on their age, gender, location, and purchasing behaviour, which can help you tailor your marketing and promotional strategies accordingly.

Marketing reports can offer a deeper understanding of the effectiveness of your marketing campaigns. By tracking the performance of your various marketing channels, such as social media, email marketing, or advertisements, you can identify what works best for your audience and optimize your marketing efforts.

Finally, financial reports can give you a detailed overview of your organization's financial health. You can track revenue, expenses, profit margins, and other financial metrics, enabling you to make informed decisions regarding budgeting and financial planning.

In summary, real-time ticketing reports can be a valuable tool for any organization that relies on ticket sales. By setting up a variety of reports that cater to your specific needs, you can stay informed and make data-driven decisions to ensure the success of your events and performances.

Reservation Software Notes

The system should be designed to allow for the attachment of conversation notes to both the client profile and the client order history. These notes should include internal history notes of the interactions at the sales level, as well as any other relevant information that may be useful to the user or the administrator.

Three types of notes should be incorporated into the system: user notes, public notes, and private notes. User notes should be attached to the client profile and used for administrative purposes to maintain the details and requirements of users. These notes should be visible to both the user and the administrator.

Public notes, on the other hand, should be text notes that an agent can enter when they are purchasing on behalf of a client. These notes should also be visible in the backend and on the order form and can be entered by the user/client when they make reservations or purchases. They should be easily changeable and updateable, ensuring that everyone involved in the transaction has access to the latest information.

Finally, private notes should only be seen in the backend and not viewable by a customer. They should be visible only to an admin agent and are meant for the admin of the site. Private notes may include sensitive information that is not intended for public viewing, such as notes on billing or shipping addresses, special requests, or other confidential information.

By incorporating these three types of notes into the system, the user and the administrator will have access to all the necessary information to complete transactions smoothly and efficiently. The use of text conversation notes will ensure that everyone involved in the transaction has access to the most up-to-date information, helping to avoid misunderstandings and errors.

Forecasting Seat Sales

In various business scenarios, there is a requirement to optimize revenue by selling a limited quantity of a perishable product. One such example is the sale of seats for a trip or voyage, where the number of seats is fixed, and they can only be sold until the departure time, after which they become obsolete. To make the most of the fixed seat inventory, ferry, bus, and airline companies need to predict demand to set prices accordingly.

Forecasting seat sales demand poses a challenge due to limited knowledge about customer preferences, and the fact that many factors influencing demand do not follow a predictable pattern. Price control serves as an effective tool in revenue management, influencing sales control and identifying the optimal pricing patterns that can maximize those sales.

For instance, one approach involves segmenting customers based on their ticket purchase timing, specifically how far in advance they bought the tickets, and correlating it with their willingness to pay. Another example pertains to short-stay vacations at a particular destination, which can be utilized in pricing and forecasting return trips. While existing forecasting models typically consider factors such as time remaining until departure and price, it is also important to take into account the round-trip price of tickets instead of focusing solely on one-way fares.

If passenger-level information is available, it becomes possible to identify significant returning flights and easily determine the major round-trip prices.

Reservation Change Management

To achieve greater operational efficiency and cost savings, it is essential to utilize advanced availability management techniques and dynamic customer identification. This includes using travel technology utilities such as auto-ticketing and schedule change management, which streamline the management of schedules.

One of the key benefits of these tools is the ability to automate the manual movement of passengers to other trips, dates, and times when weather and equipment issues force cancellations or changes in schedules. This means that travel companies can quickly adapt to unexpected circumstances and minimize disruptions to their operations.

Another important feature of these tools is the automatic notification of affected passengers by email. This provides customers with timely updates and ensures that they are informed of any changes to their travel plans.

In addition, the ability to perform automated massive schedule changes and mass move passengers from one trip/tour to another is critical for travel companies that need to make changes to their schedules on short notice. By automating these reservation tasks, travel agents can focus on providing excellent customer care and addressing any concerns or issues that arise during the travel process.

Overall, utilizing advanced availability management techniques and dynamic customer identification, along with travel technology utilities such as auto-ticketing and schedule change management, can significantly improve the efficiency and effectiveness of travel operations. This enables companies to provide a better customer experience, increase revenue, and reduce costs.

Reservation Inventory Management

The primary requirement for a large smart city traveller-centric system is to develop a comprehensive reservation system with specialized inventory management capabilities. This system should enable administrators to create, price, allocate, and modify inventory in real-time, leveraging an integrated real-time inventory management system.

Expanding upon this foundation, the system should incorporate user-defined item-level occupancy and pricing control. This means that users should have the flexibility to set specific occupancy levels and corresponding pricing for each item in the inventory. Additionally, the system should support event, category, and item-level fee assignments, allowing users to define fees at various levels of granularity.

In-depth discount calculation and application should be an integral part of the system. It should provide robust mechanisms to calculate discounts based on specific criteria and apply them accurately to relevant bookings. Furthermore, the system should facilitate online credit card transaction processing, ensuring secure and convenient payment processing for users.

To streamline event creation, the system should offer templates and the ability to clone entire events, categories, or individual items. This feature will simplify the process of setting up new events and reduce the effort required to configure similar offerings. Moreover, the system should allow the implementation of roles and permissions to define authorities and access at the individual user level. This ensures that different users have appropriate access rights and privileges within the system.

Dynamic item-level pricing should be supported, enabling the system to adjust prices based on user-defined business rules and configuration. This flexibility allows for adaptive pricing strategies that can respond to changing market conditions and demand patterns. Additionally, the system should facilitate multi-tier inventory management, allowing administrators to organize inventory into multiple tiers or levels for better categorization and control.

Dimensional pricing should be implemented to accommodate varying pricing structures based on dimensions such as size, weight, or other relevant attributes of the inventory items. This capability enables more accurate and customizable pricing models. User-defined business rules, fees, and discounts should also be supported throughout the system, allowing users to configure specific rules and policies that align with their business requirements.

In summary, a robust smart city traveller-centric system should encompass specialized inventory management, real-time inventory updates, user-defined item level occupancy and pricing control, event, category, and item level fee assignment, in-depth discount calculation and application, online credit card transaction processing, simplified event creation through templates and cloning, roles and permissions for user access control, dynamic item-level pricing based on business rules, multi-tier inventory management, dimensional pricing, and user-defined business rules, fees, and discounts.

Passenger Inventory Management

Passenger inventory management is another crucial component in the efficient operation of any transportation system. It encompasses a range of key functionalities that enable reservations and inventory control, trip and schedule management, and associated processes such as pricing, ticketing, and check-in.

To effectively manage passenger bookings, a traveller-centric reservations system must cater to various channels through which bookings are made. This includes managing bookings made at local and partner sales offices, travel distributors, and online platforms. By encompassing these diverse sources, the system ensures a seamless and comprehensive approach to passenger management.

To build a robust infrastructure for passenger management, it is essential to establish a flexible platform that incorporates core system features required by every transit company. These features typically include reservations, ticketing, inventory management, check-in, departure control, as well as weight and balance calculations. By implementing these core functionalities, the system can cater to the fundamental requirements of any transportation scenario.

The chosen solution for passenger management should possess scalability, cost-effectiveness, and adaptability. It must be able to accommodate the needs of growing carriers, providing them with the necessary building blocks for expansion. Simultaneously, it should offer well-established carriers the means to broaden their market reach and explore new opportunities. This flexibility ensures that the system can evolve and adapt to the changing demands of the transportation industry.

In addition to efficient management of passenger logistics, a traveller-centric passenger management and distribution system should incorporate technologies that optimize customer service. This includes providing online, kiosk, and mobile applications to enhance the convenience and accessibility of bookings. Self-service booking options, shopping solutions, merchandising features, and loyalty programs further enhance the overall customer experience.

To facilitate collaboration with various partners, the system should include an interface for third-party distribution. This allows seamless integration and interaction with all relevant partners, ensuring efficient communication and coordination within the transportation ecosystem.

In summary, an effective passenger inventory management system encompasses various functionalities, including reservations, inventory control, trip and schedule management, as well as pricing, ticketing, and check-in processes. It should be built on a flexible infrastructure, accommodating the needs of both growing and established carriers. The system should optimize customer service through various technologies, while also providing seamless integration with third-party partners

Create Activity Packages

In a smart city Traveller-centric reservation system with its wide variety of tourist and mobility offerings, it is envisaged that the necessity for some form of packaging would be required. As such, I offer the following minimalist design feature list.

Design Requirement: Traveller-Centric Reservation System for a Smart City

The system shall allow the administrator to create packages containing tours/trips, rooms in hotels, and products to cater to the diverse needs of travellers.

The system shall enable the creation of activity packages that consist of multiple "products," allowing the administrator to track and control inventory for each "package product" with special prices.

The system shall support the creation, scheduling, pricing, booking, and management of both one-off and series departure packages, offering flexibility to accommodate various travel itineraries.

Each package shall have the ability to include any combination of services, similar to a custom FIT itinerary, such as "rooms," "tours," "transit trips," and other "products."

The system shall provide options to customize package tours by incorporating different daily options, such as room types and hotel quality, allowing for personalized experiences.

The system shall offer the choice to save package tours with fixed pricing per person or book them using database-driven pricing to cater to different pricing strategies.

Package tours can include agent mark-up and commission structures, enabling agents to tailor the tour for individual clients or shopping groups.

An agent portal shall be incorporated into the system, providing agents with the ability to view and book packages, make payments, and generate quotation documents using their branding and logo.

The system shall provide a comprehensive suite of reports to assist in the management of package departures, including flight manifests, travel manifests (coach), rooming lists, departure lists, resort/ground handler reports, and activity allocations.

The administrator shall have the capability to select sub-elements within the product package add/edit page, allowing for customization of each package. Special options may include the ability to limit package selection within specified periods, set a minimum quantity of booked seats, and specify a minimum number of booked days.

Customers shall have the ability to enter options for each item within the package, including arrival/departure dates, number of rooms, arrival and departure date/time for tours/transit items, passenger information, and quantity for other products (e.g., food).

Upon customer selection of a package, the system shall check the availability of all items within the package by checking inventory for tours, trips, rooms, etc.

After booking a reservation package deal, the system shall update the inventory for each item within the package (e.g., room, tour, transit, and product), reflecting the changes made.

The system shall provide an easy-to-use interface for posting package tours on the website for booking, with centralized inventory control. As bookings are made, the system shall automatically track remaining availability, allowing pre-assignment of room and other allocations to the package.

Create a one-time package, which contains a simple transfer and an accommodation, but also create an advanced dynamic package with different transfers to choose from, multiple departures, various accommodations and optional or required activities. In any case, the system should make it easy for you to define all the details of your offer.

Define advanced pricing lists as travel product prices tend to be complicated because they depend on the season, passenger age, supplier discounts, etc. Now combine a few of those products into a single package, and it gets complicated.

Once you define all your and your suppliers' travel products in the system, it should automatically calculate all the prices for a tour package. It must take into account the number of passengers, the current season for each travel product; group discounts, and even dynamically recalculate prices in case of client drop-off.

Future-proofing Tourism: Embracing Smart Technologies and Software as a Service

In recent years, "software as a service" (SaaS) has become an appealing alternative to purchasing, installing, and maintaining, "modifiable off-the-shelf" (MOTS) software packages.

In part, this is due to the extensive adoption of information and communication technologies in tourism, for instance in the form of global distribution and central reservation systems following the integration of web-based technologies that led to the emergence of e–tourism.

An advantage of SaaS is that it delivers a bundle of applications and services through the web. Its on-demand features allow users to enjoy full scalability and handle possible demand fluctuations at no risk. But, the issue with SaaS is that typically it suffers from "lack-of-fit".

The inability of SaaS to readily integrate cross-application data, i.e., "lack-of-fit", puts it at a tremendous cost disadvantage with the traditional MOTS providers.

A MOTS provider, by contrast, can enhance software functionality and features, integrate with published data sets, access open information systems and business models and enable stakeholders to manage their smart tourism ecosystems dynamically and support other plugging and playing stakeholders depending on what resources need to be exchanged.

With the advent of smart cities and smart tourism, tourism firms have to collaborate with stakeholders beyond their organizational borders to source and exchange resources for value co-creation.

As many cities are now publishing data sets containing large volumes of data on points of interest, transit schedules, parking spaces, and so much more, that can be consumed and integrated into many mobile apps and other software systems, then open business ecosystems are becoming a necessity.

These enable actors to co-create value in context, by accessing, mixing and matching, exchanging, adapting and integrating resources in many different and flexible ways depending upon their consumption and monetizing situation.

As such smart tourism and transport software that uses innovative technology for content delivery to tourists and small tourism business networks that allow for plug-and-play scenarios are required to seize emerging value-creation opportunities.

The importance of mobile technology for co-creation is required in the smart tourism ecosystem, but also complex business ecosystems that create and supports the exchange of touristic resources and the co-creation of the tourism experience are required to feed these mobile devices.

A Traveller-centric system requires many individual niche modules, such as Tour, Hotel, Rental, campground, Marina, Parking, Ferry and Bus, third-party transit suppliers, etc., with eCommerce and ticketing, suitable for smart city and smart tourism websites.

These are suggested modules which can be installed together or individually on separate websites, allow interaction between websites, websites to hubs, smart city "data set" integration, supplier interactivity and the ability to monetize and deliver reservations and content to the consumer by responsive or mobile devices.

Business to Business (B2B)

General retailers have always succeeded by striking a carefully calibrated balance between offering a wide choice of goods and the opportunity cost of offering each additional category.

But customers in the savvy new generation who shop both on and off-line have different expectations of Web-based retailing: they want greater depth of inventory as well as rich and relevant online product information.

By teaming up with online category managers or wholesalers, traveller-centric retailers within that system can look forward to increasing their revenue, with little corresponding increase in stock or fulfilment costs.

This approach, which generally goes under the banner of "syndicated stores," differs significantly from ordinary category management only in that customers know they are entering a part of the site controlled by the manufacturer's brand rather than by you the host retailer.

Making sure your customers get the right products, at the right place, on time and intact is a critical part of their overall satisfaction. As is making sure their questions and issues are addressed before, during and after an order is placed and delivered. How you handle these situations determines whether you win a customer for life. Or push them in the direction of your competitors.

Sales Staff (Call Center) Desk

A Sales Staff (Call Center) Desk is also to be considered, such that allows the website owner to utilize internal Sales Staff, Sales Agent Reservations or inbound/outbound Call Center staff or Kiosk-based staff to book or make reservations on behalf of a client.

For internal staff, call centres and kiosk fulfilment service providers, it would need to offer the functionality and management of inventory, customers, and orders. Also manages sales connections, product access, reservations, payments and bookings, commissions and travel agent connections, etc.

An Order Management Software system to provide a full customer service suite to manage inbound and outbound queries, rich order management, and a dispatch hub to enable efficient order fulfilment for all client sales channels. Your back office systems can then be fully integrated into your website to enable both upstream and downstream data flow, all in real time.

Leveraging a common inventory shared across online marketplaces and sales channels will help reduce over-bookings and grow profits. Leverage further your tours or accommodation, transit trips, rentals and product sales with cross and up-sells to increase the lifetime average order transaction value of each of your or your client's customers.

Sales Staff should be allowed to create a new customer or third-party profile or use a client's existing customer profile from the main client database.

Even though you have or are thinking of moving online for taking reservations, you will still be receiving requests by telephone, fax or email. Also, depending upon the type of services you offer, you will be required to answer walk-up, front desk, bus stop, onboard or dockside, etc., reservation questions.

This requires your sales staff to not only have the ability to be connected to your online reservation software but also can make bookings, amend bookings, scan tickets, etc., etc.

Ticket Kiosks

Set up one or more kiosks using any modern tablet or other kiosk system and use this new feature to provide users with a convenient check-in experience for those not accustomed to using apps...

Registration delays and data entry errors can be alleviated by allowing users to enter or confirm their information for themselves.

An after-hours kiosk will let users find their reservation, check in and receive the information they need for their bookings. Even users without a reservation can check availability, make reservations and make a payment directly from your kiosk.

Sales Staff Features for Sales Agent Reservations

Consider providing the ability for your sales staff to be assigned their unique username and password to log into the reservation system.

They are then able to access their own sales area.

Your sales staff can make bookings for clients, create new profiles for new clients or book under their own unique sales staff ID.

Provide the ability to select any applicable booking etc., by day, date period, time and view what is available and then make an appropriate booking according to the customer's request.

Allow the taking of deposits; full payments also cash payments and vouchers, and coupons for walk-ups, kiosks or on-board traffic.

Where applicable, allow ticket barcode scanning for your sales staff, drivers, etc., as a standard feature.

You can also allow your sales staff to modify and cancel orders, upgrade orders, and even transfer clients from equipment to other equipment, etc.

Sales staff may also assign rooms or cabins, etc., to clients.

You can pay your staff commissions, following hours that staff have worked, assign staff or captains and mates or drivers to equipment, trips, etc.

Consider compensation to staff with "Multiple Commission Structures". Allow stake owners to create Reseller (Travel Agent) groups and assign them different or unique commission rates.

As such, you can create unique commission groups to assign your sales staff or agents. Each commission group can have its commission structure. This enables you to reward "high performers", "managers and executives", or even create "special terms bonus" agents.

Agent Administration & Reporting – Allow Managers to control all Staff/Resellers assigned in their system. Owners/Administrators can select the display for reporting periods, with details such as Order number, Order date, Payment method, Total amount, Status of order, Sales Staff commission rate and Commission amounts being available. This report can also be used as a commission statement.

This allows Sales Staff to take orders by telephone, a kiosk, fax or email and enter them directly into the system via their browser to create reservations, print tickets or make bookings using the client profile selected from the client list.

All integrated information should be made available for call centre reservation staff to answer phone reservations: rates, availability, and package or event availability. Access would need to be timely and accurately brought up to best serve the client, from the pre-purchase stage.

An integrated Sales Staff/Call Center module can also accommodate phone reservations from travel agents and corporate clients. Integrated accordingly, sales staff will view negotiated contract rates and allotments assigned to particular staff or corporate customers.

Traveller-centric Shoppers & Shopper Groups

Consider the use of creating shopper groups and assigning them to registered users.

Within shopper groups, you can offer different products or prices to different users.

People who are visiting your website are either visitors or registered users.

Depending on your configuration they can create a user account without buying anything.

Usually, after they purchase the first product or booking, they are a registered user on your website, although with Traveller-centric systems you can set up Guest privileges and not require sign-up.

This enables administrators to create Shopper Groups for whatever need (e.g. access control, personalization and e-commerce management, customer rating, tax display, vendor, supplier, etc.).

These shopper groups can then be used to provide special services, discounts, or access to a specific group of users.

Depending on your site configuration they can either create a user account without buying anything or the account will be created automatically when the first order is placed.

Administrators can create shopper groups and assign them to registered users or create one for non-registered visitors.

Why assign shoppers to the shopper group? With shopper groups, you can offer different products or prices to different users.

Such as making certain bookings available only for predefined user groups. For example, Platinum member users will have access to certain selected products.

Also, create discounts on each product for members of certain groups.

Finally, create a special reduced price for single products or packages for users from specified groups.

Social Networking

Integrating social media into a traveller-centric reservation and booking system for a smart city can enhance the overall user experience and provide various benefits. Here are some ideas on how you can utilize and integrate social media into such a system:

Social Login and Profile Integration: Allow users to log in or sign up using their social media accounts. This simplifies the registration process and allows users to import their profile information, such as name, profile picture, and contact details, directly from their social media accounts.

Social Sharing and Recommendations: Enable users to share their travel plans, bookings, and experiences on social media platforms. Incorporate social sharing buttons within the reservation system, allowing users to share their bookings or recommend specific destinations, accommodations, or activities to their social networks. This can help in generating buzz and attract more travellers to the smart city.

User Reviews and Ratings: Integrate social media reviews and ratings for accommodations, restaurants, attractions, and other services within the booking system. This allows travellers to view feedback from other users, promoting transparency and aiding in decision-making.

Influencer Partnerships: Collaborate with social media influencers who specialize in travel or the specific smart city. Partnering with influencers can increase brand awareness, reach a wider audience, and encourage travellers to utilize the reservation and booking system. You can offer influencers exclusive discounts, upgrades, or personalized experiences in exchange for promoting the system on their social media platforms.

User-Generated Content: Encourage travellers to share their photos, videos, and stories related to their experiences in the smart city. Create a dedicated hashtag for the smart city and integrate a social media feed within the reservation system to showcase user-generated content. This helps in building a sense of community, inspiring other travellers, and providing authentic content for potential visitors.

Real-Time Social Media Monitoring: Monitor social media platforms for mentions, tags, or hashtags related to the smart city and its offerings. Use social listening tools to identify trends, gather feedback, and address any customer service issues promptly. This allows you to stay engaged with travellers, respond to queries, and provide personalized recommendations or assistance.

Social Media Contests and Giveaways: Organize contests or giveaways on social media platforms to engage with travellers and promote the reservation system. For example, you can run a photo contest where users share their best travel moments in the smart city, with prizes that include discounts or freebies for their next bookings through the system.

Personalized Recommendations: Utilize social media data and user preferences to offer personalized recommendations to travellers. Analyze their social media profiles, interests, and connections to suggest relevant accommodations, activities, or events in the smart city. This enhances the user experience by providing tailored suggestions based on their social media footprint.

Social Media Customer Support: Integrate social media channels into your customer support system. Allow travellers to ask questions, make inquiries, or report issues directly through social media platforms. Provide timely responses and resolutions, ensuring excellent customer service and building a positive reputation for the reservation system.

Social Analytics and Insights: Leverage social media analytics to gather insights about traveller behaviour, preferences, and trends. Analyze data related to social media engagement, conversions, and sentiment to refine marketing strategies, improve the reservation system, and optimize the traveller experience.

Remember to consider privacy concerns and ensure compliance with applicable data protection regulations when integrating social media into your reservation and booking system.

Tax Capabilities

The system will require a Tax module for a wide range of tax situations

Integrating a tax module into a smart city traveller-centric reservation and booking system involves several steps. Here's a general outline of the process:

Understand Tax Regulations: Start by familiarizing yourself with the tax regulations applicable to the smart city or the region where the system will be deployed. Different jurisdictions may have different tax rules and rates for various services, such as accommodation, transportation, or entertainment. It's essential to gather accurate information about the specific taxes that need to be incorporated into the system.

Identify Taxable Services: Determine which services within the reservation and booking system are subject to taxation. This could include hotel accommodations, car rentals, tour packages, transport, parking or any other services offered through the system. Make a comprehensive list of taxable services based on the tax regulations you have researched.

Determine Tax Calculation Method: Once you have identified the taxable services, you need to determine how taxes will be calculated. Tax calculations can vary based on factors such as the type of service, the location of the transaction, or the customer's residency. Common tax calculation methods include flat rates, percentage-based rates, or a combination of both. Consult with tax professionals or local authorities to ensure accurate tax calculations.

Modify Pricing Structure: Adjust the pricing structure of the reservation and booking system to accommodate taxes. Taxes are typically added to the base price of the service. Update the system's database or backend to store the tax information for each service, including the tax rate and any applicable exemptions or thresholds.

Implement Tax Calculation Logic: Develop or modify the system's code to incorporate the tax calculation logic. This may involve integrating an external tax calculation API or implementing custom tax calculation algorithms within the system. Ensure that the tax calculation takes into account the relevant factors such as the service type, location, and customer information.

Display Tax Information: Update the user interface of the reservation and booking system to display tax information transparently to users. This may include showing the tax amount separately or as part of the total price during the booking process. Communicate to users which services are taxable and provide details about the taxes applied.

Generate Tax Reports: Implement functionality to generate tax reports for administrative purposes. This will enable the system administrators to review and audit the tax transactions and ensure compliance. The reports should provide detailed information about the taxable services, tax amounts, and any other relevant data required by the tax authorities.

Testing and Compliance: Thoroughly test the integration of the tax module within the system to ensure accurate tax calculations and proper functioning. Verify that the tax calculations align with the tax regulations and conduct real-world testing scenarios to identify any potential issues. Work closely with tax professionals or local authorities to ensure compliance with the tax laws and regulations.

Ongoing Maintenance and Updates: Tax regulations can change over time, so it's important to monitor any updates and make necessary adjustments to the tax module accordingly. Stay informed about changes in tax rates, exemptions, or any other relevant tax-related factors that may affect the system. Regularly update the tax module to reflect these changes and perform maintenance tasks as required.

Remember, tax integration can be complex, and it's advisable to consult with tax professionals or legal experts who specialize in the specific jurisdiction to ensure accurate implementation and compliance with local tax laws.

Live Chat Feature

A powerful instant text messaging 'Live Chat' application feature for customers, travel agents/resellers, internal sales and administration is also advantageous within the system

By optimizing how you connect with your online customers with our integrated live chat, you can sell to more of your website visitors, raise the average value of the orders they place there, and keep them coming back to buy more from your site.

A Real-time live chat feature alternative to phone and e-mail and no need to purchase or rent an external live chat program.

Expedite the booking process. Adding a live chat feature or click-to-call button on your website lets travellers book and confirm their trips immediately.

Save the reservation. Immediately answering customers' questions can prevent abandonment.

Engage luxury customers. Reaching out to customers who pause on a luxury resort page and whose profiles indicate they frequent these destinations up the likelihood of conversion.

Identify and target high-value visitors. Integrating the sales and client profile data from the system helps you target, e.g., a customer who regularly books employee incentive and reward trips for large corporations with a customized air and hotel bundle.

Build consumer confidence by assisting with complex product and service decisions.

Reduce costs. Shifting requests from the telephone to more cost-effective online channels allows your agents to complete more bookings and resolve more service issues in less time.

Foster long-term customer loyalty and satisfaction.

Providing online personal assistance to the right customer at the right time drives acquisition, satisfaction, and retention in today's competitive travel environment.

Redefining Travel Experiences: Architecting a Traveller-Centric System for Smart Cities

Designing and building a smart city traveller-centric booking and reservation system using PHP and MySQL is a feasible approach. Here's an overview of the advantages and disadvantages, as well as some alternative solutions to consider:

Advantages of PHP and MySQL:

Widely used: PHP is a popular scripting language for web development, and MySQL is a widely adopted relational database management system (RDBMS). There is a large community and abundant resources available for support and troubleshooting.

Web compatibility: PHP is specifically designed for web development, making it suitable for building web-based booking systems. MySQL integrates seamlessly with PHP, allowing efficient data storage and retrieval.

Flexibility: PHP offers flexibility in terms of integration with various frameworks, libraries, and APIs, allowing you to leverage existing tools and services.

Scalability: PHP and MySQL can handle large amounts of data and can scale as the user base of your booking system grows.

Disadvantages of PHP and MySQL:

Security vulnerabilities: PHP has been criticized for security concerns in the past. However, with proper coding practices and security measures, these risks can be mitigated.

Performance limitations: While PHP is generally fast, it may not be the most performant option for certain complex operations. However, optimizing code and database queries can help overcome performance limitations.

Learning curve: If you're not already familiar with PHP and MySQL, there may be a learning curve involved in mastering these technologies.

Alternative Solutions:

Node.js and MongoDB: Node.js is a JavaScript runtime built on Chrome's V8 engine, and MongoDB is a NoSQL database. This combination can provide high scalability and real-time capabilities, making it suitable for handling large amounts of data and concurrent users.

Ruby on Rails and PostgreSQL: Ruby on Rails is a popular web development framework, and PostgreSQL is a robust open-source relational database. This combination offers a productive development environment and strong data consistency.

Django and PostgreSQL: Django is a high-level Python web framework, and PostgreSQL is a reliable RDBMS. Django's batteries-included approach and PostgreSQL's advanced features make it a powerful combination for building complex systems.

Creating a traveller-centric website that integrates with multiple APIs and uses a MySQL database requires careful planning and execution.

Website Design:

Identify the core features: Determine the primary functionalities of your traveller-centric website. These could include flight and hotel bookings, itinerary planning, travel recommendations, reviews, user profiles, and social interactions.

Choose the appropriate APIs: Research and select the APIs that provide the necessary data and services for your website. Consider APIs for flights, hotels, car rentals, weather forecasts, maps, payment gateways, and social media integration. Ensure that these APIs offer machine-to-machine (M2M) and business-to-business (B2B) capabilities.

Database design: Create a MySQL database schema to store all the relevant data for your website. Identify the entities and their relationships, and design appropriate tables to represent them. For example, you may have tables for users, bookings, itineraries, reviews, and more. Normalize your database structure to eliminate redundancy and improve efficiency.

API integration: Develop the necessary backend code to integrate with the selected APIs. Use the APIs' documentation and SDKs to handle authentication, requests, and responses. Implement functions to retrieve data such as flight availability, hotel details, and booking information.

User interface design: Design an intuitive and user-friendly interface for your website. Consider the user journey and ensure that the key features are easily accessible. Use modern web technologies like HTML5, CSS3, and JavaScript frameworks (e.g., React, Angular, or Vue.js) to build a responsive and interactive front.

Backend development: Develop the backend of your website using a server-side language such as Node.js, Python, or PHP. Build APIs and endpoints to handle user requests and interact with the database. Implement business logic, data validation, and error handling.

User authentication and security: Implement a robust user authentication system to secure user data and prevent unauthorized access. Utilize technologies like JSON Web Tokens (JWT) or OAuth for user authentication and authorization. Apply best practices for password hashing and storage.

Payment gateway integration: If your website involves financial transactions, integrate a reliable payment gateway API to handle secure payments. Ensure compliance with relevant security standards such as Payment Card Industry Data Security Standard (PCI DSS).

Testing and quality assurance: Conduct thorough testing of your website to identify and fix any bugs or issues. Perform functional testing, integration testing, and usability testing to ensure a smooth user experience. Optimize the performance of your website and validate its compatibility across different devices and browsers.

Deployment and maintenance: Deploy your website to a reliable hosting platform or server. Configure backups, monitoring, and security measures to maintain the website's stability and availability. Regularly update and maintain the software components, including API integrations and security patches.

Analytics and continuous improvement: Integrate analytics tools to gather insights into user behaviour, preferences, and website performance. Utilize this data to make data-driven decisions and continuously improve your website's functionality and user experience.

Remember, developing a traveller-centric website with API integrations is a complex task that may require the expertise of web developers, database administrators, and UI/UX designers. Additionally, consider compliance with data protection regulations and privacy policies while handling user data.

It's important to stay up-to-date with the latest technology trends, security practices, and API updates to ensure the long-term success of your website.

Ultimately, the choice of technology depends on your specific requirements, team expertise, and project constraints. Consider factors such as scalability, performance, security, and the availability of resources and libraries when making your decision.

Connecting Smart Cities: Collaboration Via API, XML, and M2M Technologies in Mobile Systems

In the era of digital transformation, the concept of smart cities has gained significant traction. These cities harness the power of technology and data to improve the quality of life for residents, enhance sustainability, and optimize urban operations. One crucial aspect of smart city development is the integration of various technologies, including Application Programming Interfaces (APIs), Extensible Markup Language (XML), and Machine-to-Machine (M2M) communication. The following explores the role of APIs, XML, and M2M technologies in a smart city software mobile system and how they contribute to the realization of efficient, interconnected urban environments.

APIs: Enabling Seamless Integration APIs serve as the backbone of modern software systems, allowing different applications and services to communicate and exchange information. In the context of smart cities, APIs play a vital role in integrating diverse systems and data sources. By exposing specific functionalities or data sets, APIs enable seamless interoperability between various smart city components, such as transportation systems, energy grids, public safety services, and environmental monitoring.

Through APIs, a smart city mobile system can access real-time data from different sources, including traffic sensors, weather stations, parking management systems, and IoT devices. For example, a mobile application could leverage an API to retrieve information about available parking spaces, public transit schedules, or air quality indexes. By aggregating and presenting this data to users, the mobile system enhances urban mobility, reduces congestion, and promotes sustainable transportation choices.

XML: Standardizing Data Exchange XML, a markup language designed to encode documents in a format that is both human-readable and machine-readable, plays a crucial role in facilitating data exchange within a smart city mobile system. XML provides a flexible and extensible framework for structuring and organizing diverse data types, making it easier to share information across different platforms and applications.

In a smart city context, XML can be used to represent and transmit various data formats, including geospatial data, sensor readings, and citizen feedback. For instance, a mobile system can use XML to exchange information between a traffic management application and a public transportation system. XML's standardized format ensures compatibility and simplifies the integration process, allowing different stakeholders to collaborate effectively and build interconnected systems.

M2M Technologies: Enabling Autonomous Communication Machine-to-Machine (M2M) communication refers to the direct exchange of data between devices or machines without human intervention. M2M technologies, such as wireless sensors, RFID tags, and embedded systems, play a vital role in enabling the Internet of Things (IoT) within smart city environments.

In a smart city mobile system, M2M technologies facilitate the collection, transmission, and analysis of real-time data. For example, smart parking systems can utilize M2M communication to detect the availability of parking spaces and transmit this information to a mobile application. Similarly, environmental monitoring devices can use M2M technologies to relay pollution levels or weather conditions, allowing citizens to make informed decisions about their activities.

By leveraging M2M technologies, a smart city mobile system becomes a hub for gathering and disseminating information, enabling data-driven decision-making and enhancing the overall efficiency and sustainability of urban services.

As shown, APIs, XML, and M2M technologies can play instrumental roles in the development of smart city software mobile systems. These technologies enable the seamless integration of diverse urban systems, facilitate standardized data exchange, and empower autonomous communication between devices. By leveraging APIs, a smart city mobile system can access real-time data from various sources, enhancing urban mobility, safety, and sustainability. XML ensures interoperability and simplifies data exchange, while M2M technologies enable the collection and transmission of data, fostering an interconnected urban environment. As smart cities continue to evolve, the utilization of

As smart cities continue to evolve, the utilization of APIs, XML, and M2M technologies will be critical in creating integrated and efficient urban environments. These technologies enable the development of smart city software mobile systems that can enhance urban mobility, safety, and sustainability by harnessing real-time data and enabling seamless communication between devices. The ability to access and integrate diverse data sources through APIs, exchange data in a standardized format with XML, and foster autonomous communication with M2M technologies will drive the advancement of smart cities, leading to improved quality of life for residents and more sustainable urban development.

Smart Partner Connections

By using the aforementioned technologies it would be advantageous to develop a range of communications sub-systems that allow an unlimited number of inventory owners to be managed from a single administrative back-end.

Such as developing a portal that adds further capabilities by allowing an unlimited number of licensed websites to log in directly to their secure administrative area and effect changes online at their convenience in response to seasonality and market conditions.

A suggestion would be an OTA (OpenTravelTM Alliance) compliant XML web services based Reservation Data Exchange Switch. It would need to be fully scalable and easily configurable. Able to provide Web Portals with the ability to bundle XML requests to multiple suppliers in a single request, and aggregate and consume XML or any form of online data from suppliers.

For suppliers, it enables them to expose their Inventory System / CRS as OTA-compliant Web Services cost-effectively and securely giving them a wider reach.

By also applying business rules and real-time database interconnection links between multiple resellers with other applications, warehouses, manufacturers or other channel partners it allows client websites to dynamically retrieve data as needed, just as if there were a persistent server connection.

This would be ideal for companies requiring an Internet-based enterprise-wide reservations software system sharing real-time files and data at unlimited local or remote websites.

A Smart City Traveller-centric distribution strategy should take this functionality upwards to a whole new level with extended partner capabilities, and also provide the ability to share its database with multiple "Satellite" or 'Child' versions of the central system. This allows client websites to have the fully functioned satellite version of the central system run on their website sharing data directly via a communication sub-system within the main central database, as well as the standard features.

Integrating with the "Internet of Things" (IoT)

It should be noted that integration with "The Internet of Things" (IoT) a generic term that is a vast network of physical objects embedded with advanced technology that enables them to communicate, sense their surroundings, and interact with both their internal states and the external environment. The convergence of efficient wireless protocols, enhanced sensors, affordable processors, and a plethora of innovative start-ups and established companies has propelled the concept of IoT into the mainstream. This paradigm shift from closed systems to open systems, platforms, and integrated environments presents a significant challenge for most existing reservation and booking software available today.

A Traveller-centric system specifically designed from its inception as an open-source solution and seamlessly integrating with new software, smartphones, and devices, as well as accommodating multiple application software and potential newcomers in the market, would by its nature enable the development of a dynamic and interconnected network of IoT devices.

Utilizing a PHP and MySQL platform, such a Traveller-centric system possesses virtually limitless scalability. It can function as a stand-alone website-hosted solution for smaller clients or expand to a multi-tenant, multi-client configuration. Leveraging the power of the cloud, it needs to be equipped to support a global infrastructure, enabling the creation of new services and empowering individuals worldwide to generate content and applications.

Via a variety of apps, users should be able to effortlessly connect to this global infrastructure from anywhere at any time. This becomes especially relevant in the context of Smart City operations, where companies seek to connect their tour reservation and booking websites with the broader market and collaborate with other services and government agencies to expand their businesses. A Traveller-centric system transforms into a globally accessible network of interconnected things, users, and consumers who can contribute content, avail themselves of additional business opportunities, and access a wide array of new services and bookings.

Within the framework of IoT advancements, users can leverage various sensor devices to monitor vehicle locations, client ID bracelets, mobile ticketing, seat reservation selections, parking space availability, and much more. The continuous development of IoT implies that environments, cities, buildings, vehicles, portable devices, and other objects are increasingly associated with a wealth of information and possess the ability to sense, communicate, network, and generate new data.

With such an open architecture, open-source nature, and commitment to ongoing and scalable development, Traveller-centric seamlessly supports business models that extend beyond the boundaries of individual companies. Instead, it facilitates the creation of highly dynamic networks of companies and new value chains, transforming the landscape of the reservation and booking industry.

Epilogue: Envisioning the Future

In conclusion, the development and implementation of a smart city traveller-centric software system that provides reservation and ticketing capabilities for various aspects of travel, including tours, mobility, transit tourism, parking, restaurants, and hotels, via apps, websites, and other digital platforms, would revolutionize the way people experience and navigate cities.

By leveraging the power of technology and data, this software system would offer numerous benefits to both travellers and the city itself. For travellers, it can provide convenience, efficiency, and a seamless travel experience. They would have the ability to plan and book their entire itinerary from a single platform, saving time and effort. The system would offer real-time information on availability, prices, and options, empowering travellers to make informed decisions and customize their experiences according to their preferences.

The reservation and ticketing capabilities would extend to various aspects of travel, ensuring a comprehensive solution for travellers. They could easily book guided tours to explore the city's landmarks and attractions, reserve tickets for public transportation or specialized transit tourism experiences, secure parking spots in advance, and make restaurant and hotel reservations, all within the same user-friendly system.

Moreover, this software system would benefit the city by optimizing resource allocation, enhancing the overall tourist experience, and promoting sustainable practices. Integrating with the city's transportation infrastructure would help manage the flow of tourists, reducing congestion and enhancing mobility. Real-time data on parking availability and usage would allow for efficient management of parking spaces, minimizing traffic congestion and pollution.

Additionally, the system would enable the city to gather valuable insights and data on traveller preferences, behaviour patterns, and trends. This information could be leveraged to make data-driven decisions for urban planning, infrastructure development, and tourism management. The city could identify popular attractions, understand peak visiting hours, and allocate resources accordingly, improving the overall tourist experience and ensuring a positive perception of the city as a tourist destination.

Furthermore, by streamlining the reservation and ticketing process, the software system would reduce the reliance on physical infrastructure, such as ticket counters and information centres, leading to cost savings and increased operational efficiency for both travellers and service providers. It would also foster collaboration between different stakeholders, including tour operators, transportation companies, parking providers, and hospitality businesses, by providing a centralized platform for communication and coordination.

However, it is essential to address potential challenges such as data security, and privacy concerns, and ensure inclusivity in the adoption of such a system. Implementing robust security measures, complying with data protection regulations, and ensuring accessibility for all users, regardless of their digital literacy or access to technology, would be crucial considerations in developing and deploying the software system.

In summary, a smart city traveller-centric software system with reservation and ticketing capabilities has the potential to transform the way travellers interact with cities. Offering convenience, efficiency, and personalized experiences, would enhance the overall travel experience for tourists while promoting sustainable practices and optimizing resource allocation for the city. With careful planning, collaboration, and addressing potential challenges, the system envisaged and outlined in this missive can contribute to the development of smarter, more visitor-friendly cities.

John Shenton - June 2023

Don't miss out!

Visit the website below and you can sign up to receive emails whenever John Shenton publishes a new book. There's no charge and no obligation.

https://books2read.com/r/B-A-RJUO-UTNJC

BOOKS 2 READ

Connecting independent readers to independent writers.

Did you love *The Smart City Odyssey: Unveiling the Secrets to Traveller-Centric Software*? Then you should read *The Bahamas - More Islands and Recipes Than You Expect!*[1] by John Shenton!

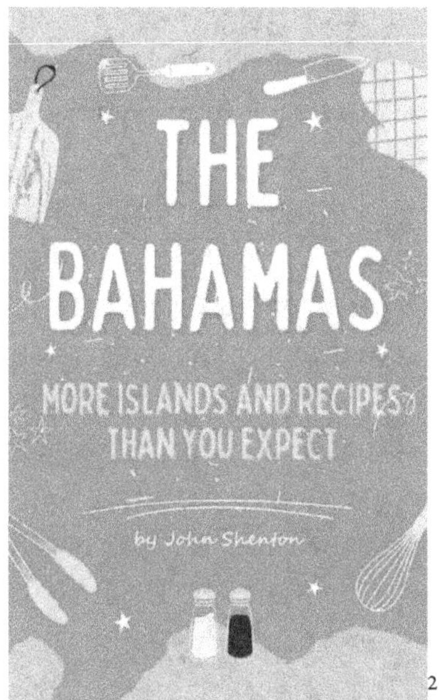

Welcome to the Bahama Islands history and cuisine!

Enjoy a romantic vacation in the Bahamas! But there's another world out there beyond the major tourist destinations just waiting to be discovered: The Out Islands of Abaco, Andros, the Berry Islands, Bimini, Cat Island, Crooked Island, Eleuthera, the Exumas, Harbour Island, Long Island, and so on.

The Out Islands have long been a popular destination for sailors, sport fishermen and divers...

Visitors to the Bahamas soon discover that instead of arriving at one destination, they have stumbled upon many!

---

1. https://books2read.com/u/3n7Pde

2. https://books2read.com/u/3n7Pde

Just 50 miles off the Florida coast, the islands of the Bahamas are as diverse as they are lovely. The bustling marketplaces, marinas, and hotels of Freeport and Nassau seem worlds away from the pine forests and mangrove swamps of the Lucayan National Park.

The more cosmopolitan islands provide traditional tourist fare, but others offer secluded beaches, tiny palm-lined villages, and stalagmite-filled caves. Stretching from Grand Bahama and Abaco at the north to Great Inagua at the south are 23 inhabited islands and hundreds of uninhabited islands and cays (pronounced "keys"). With six distinct ecosystems and many different adventures to be had, the islands of the Bahamas offer visitors a paradise of possibilities.

This book also includes over 50 Simple-To-Cook Recipes and features Fritters and more fritters, Bahamian Ham & Banana Mix, Island Minced Pie, Rumball Cookies, Boiled Fish, Johnny Cake, Goombay Smash, and many more favourites "from the islands of ocean blue where Columbus landed in 1492." Although virtually any type of international food can be found in The Islands of The Bahamas, it would be a mistake to miss an opportunity to sample the local cuisine. No matter where you are, you won't have any difficulty finding plenty of restaurants serving Bahamian cuisine and fresh local seafood at reasonable prices. The cuisine of The Islands of The Bahamas is never, ever bland. Spicy, subtly and uniquely flavoured with local meats and produce, more than any other cuisine in the West Indies, Bahamian cooking has been influenced by the American South.

The light, luscious, tropical, and healthy Bahamian cuisine derives from seafood, which is a principal industry as well as a local food staple. Nourished and supported by the local catch for centuries, the Bahamians have perfected a spicy cuisine using their traditional conch, grouper, crawfish, pigeon peas, breadfruit, guava, mango, and a variety of hot pepper sauces.

The conch, pronounced 'konk', is served, cooked or uncooked, in chowders or fritters, or added to soups, salads, and stews. Other delicacies include land crabs and local spiny lobsters, which are boiled, baked or steamed and served with pigeon peas, rice or grits, or minced into salads and soups. Popular dishes also include boil fish served with grits and stew fish served with vegetables.

Try some of these recipes for a taste of the Bahamas at home.

Also by John Shenton

Business Plan Basics
The Bahamas - More Islands and Recipes Than You Expect!
Collected Musings from Bricks and Mortar to E-commerce
The Smart City Odyssey: Unveiling the Secrets to Traveller-Centric
Software
The Dragon's Gambit: China's Bid for Global Dominance and the
Western Response
Silent Weapon
Business Basics: Money Sources
Influx
Fried Chips
Mandates, Motors, and Misinformation
Echos of Orwell
Control and Chaos
The Empire's Warning: What Rome's Fall Tells Us About the West
Today

About the Author

John Shenton was born in Birmingham, England and grew up in postwar England. He spent several years as a Radio Officer onboard a variety of vessels sailing to the Persian Gulf, the Indian Ocean and South China seas.

With degrees and a background in electronics and computers he has lived and worked within the United Kingdom, Germany, Switzerland and Canada.

While doing so, he established numerous trading relationships in Japan, Korea, the USA, China and other countries.

He has been retired for some time now living in Montréal Canada enjoying golfing, writing, sailing and many other things automotive.

About the Publisher

John Shenton published via Draft2digital